WORKING
IT
OUT

A Troubleshooting Guide
for Writers

WORKING
IT
OUT

✍

A Troubleshooting Guide
for Writers

Second Edition

✍

BARBARA FINE CLOUSE

The McGraw-Hill Companies, Inc.
New York   St. Louis   San Francisco   Auckland   Bogotá   Caracas   Lisbon
London   Madrid   Mexico City   Milan   Montreal   New Delhi
San Juan   Singapore   Sydney   Tokyo   Toronto

McGraw-Hill
*A Division of The **McGraw-Hill** Companies*

This book was set in Melior by Graphic World, Inc.
The editors were Tim Julet, Laura Lynch, and Jean Akers;
the production supervisor was Richard A. Ausburn;
the designer was Karen Quigley.
Quebecor Printing/Fairfield Graphics was printer and binder.

WORKING IT OUT
A Troubleshooting Guide for Writers

This book is printed on acid-free paper.

1 2 3 4 5 6 7 8 9 0 FGR FGR 9 0 9 8 7 6 5

ISBN 0-07-011619-9

Library of Congress Cataloging-in-Publication Data

Clouse, Barbara Fine.
  Working it out: a troubleshooting guide for
writers/Barbara Fine Clouse.—2nd ed.
      p.   cm.
  Includes index.
  ISBN 0-07-011619-9
  1. Authorship   I. Title.
PN145.c64 1997
808'.02—dc20   96-12975

In loving memory of Bob Krantz

Contents

Contents ✔

APPENDIXES   149

Preface

Working It Out: A Troubleshooting Guide for Writers is a compendium of strategies for handling the various phases of writing: idea generation, outlining, drafting, revising, and editing. It is based on the simple belief that people write better when they discover procedures that work well for them. Thus, one goal of the book is to provide a range of strategies for writers to sample as they work to develop successful writing processes.

A second goal of the book is to provide writers with aid and comfort when they get stuck. While seasoned writers understand that false starts, wrong turns, and writer's block are all part of the process, the less-experienced may become frustrated and discouraged when their work does not proceed smoothly, especially if they do not know what to do when they hit a snag. As a troubleshooting guide, *Working It Out* provides specific strategies for dealing with writing problems. Thus, a writer who gets stuck along the way can consult the text and get the help needed to reduce frustration and move forward.

FEATURES

The features of *Working It Out* are aimed at making the book as useful as possible to those who want to improve their writing by discovering effective, efficient procedures and problem-solving strategies. These features include:

Clear, Jargon-free Prose Written in a Conversational Style

So the book can be a ready reference both in and out of the classroom, explanations are as brief as possible and are written in a supportive, nonintimidating, noncondescending style.

Organization across the Sequence of the Writing Process

So writers can use the text in the same sequence as the progression of their writing. Part 1 treats prewriting; Part 2 treats drafting; Part 3 treats revising; and Part 4 treats editing. (Part 5 provides topics for writing practice.)

Most Chapters Are Titled with a Question or Remark Frequently Voiced by Student Writers

This way, students and other novice writers can find what they need faster because chapter titles echo their own language and concerns.

Over 190 Helpful Strategies

There are enough specific suggestions here that all users should find many ways to solve problems and improve their writing processes.

Computer Strategies

A range of strategies is offered for those who favor writing at the computer.

An Overview of the Writing Process and Essay Structure

Chapter 1 contains information on the stages of the writing process; the writer's audience, purpose, and role; essay structure; and how to become a better writer.

A Process Log and Reader Response Questionnaire

Appendix 1 shows writers how to use a process log to monitor the development and facilitate the improvement of their writing processes. Appendix 2 shows writers how to use a questionnaire to learn how readers react to their drafts and what revisions are needed.

Ideas for Writing

Chapter 24 contains fifteen ideas for writing in full rhetorical context.

NEW TO THE SECOND EDITION

In response to suggestions made by reviewers and frequent users of *Working It Out*, the following changes were made for the second edition:

- Twenty-eight new strategies are included.
- The essay structure illustration was replaced with a more analytical essay model.
- The preface and Chapter 1 were reorganized for easier use. Some of this material is now in a special section entitled "How to Use This Book: A Preface to the Student."
- A number of experiential examples were replaced with nonexperiential ones.
- A chapter to help writers who discover their drafts are too long is included.
- A chapter on commas is included.
- A chapter on apostrophes is included.
- An appendix on taking essay examinations is included.
- A distinction is made between comma splices and run-on sentences.
- A strategy for choosing between *who* and *whom* is included.
- Common myths about writing are included.

Acknowledgments

I am grateful to Lesley Denton of McGraw-Hill for her willingness to publish something new and for her guidance along the way, to Tim Julet, English Editor, for his continued support, and to Laura Lynch, Associate Editor, for her attentiveness, good sense, and good humor. I am also indebted to my colleague, Jim Strickland of Slippery Rock University, who helped me with the computer strategies. To Jean Akers, editing supervisor extraordinaire, I offer profound appreciation for her sensitive reading and gentle touch. In addition, I owe much to the sound counsel offered by those who reviewed the book, both in the first edition, and in preparation for this revision: Carol Adams, Delaware Technical and Community College; Michael Allen, Northwest Missouri State University; Ken Autrey, Francis Marion College; Liz Buckley, East Texas State University; Catherine Cardwell, Youngstown State University; Barbara Daniel, Penn State University; John Daughtrey, Orange Coast Community College; Linda Donahue, Mattatuck Community College; John Green, Salem State College; Paula Gibson, Cardinal Stritch College; Bettie Horne, Lander College; Nancy Marcy, Three Rivers Community-Technical College; Richard Prystowsky, Irvine Valley College; Ann M. Salak, Cleveland State University; Susan Schmeling, Vincenness University; Rod Siegfried, American River College; Ann Pope Stone, Santa Monica College; Stuart Tichenor, Oklahoma State University; and William Woods, Wichita State University.

Finally, to Denny, Greg, and Jeff, my indulgent, understanding husband and children, I offer my heartfelt thanks for the support and for the room of my own.

Barbara Fine Clouse

A Preface to the Student: How to Use This Book

Pretend for a moment that you are on the tennis team and that you are having trouble with your baseline shots. The coach, noticing your problem, might suggest that you drop your hip a little. Now pretend that you are on the track team and you are having trouble improving your time in the 1,600-meter run. In this case, your coach might suggest that you swing your arms more and pretend a giant hand is on your back pushing you along. That's what coaches do: They make suggestions to help you solve problems that arise as a natural part of learning to do something better.

Right now, you are working to become a better writer, and as you do so, problems will arise from time to time. Do not let these problems worry you, for they are a natural part of the learning process. Whenever we try to learn something, we hit snags now and then. The point is that we need to discover how to *solve* problems—and that is a learning experience of its own.

As you work to become a better writer, think of this book as one of your coaches. If you encounter a problem, you can look to this book for one or more suggestions for solving that problem. Of course, this book is not your only coach. Your classroom teacher is the best coach of all, and your classmates and the tutors in the writing center are also good sources of information. So if you have a problem, you can also talk to one of these people to get suggestions for overcoming the obstacle. Ask them what specific procedures they follow, and try some of them to see if they work well for you too.

To use this book efficiently, do the following:

- Read over the table of contents so you have a sense of what the book covers. Notice that most of the chapters are titled with a remark often spoken by struggling writers.

- If you get stuck when you are writing, go back to the table of contents and find the remark that best expresses the problem you are having. Turn to the chapter titled with that remark.

- Quickly read the chapter (it will be short), and notice that a number of procedures are described for helping you overcome the obstacle in question. Pick the procedure that appeals to you the most and try it. If your problem is solved, great. If not, try another procedure. (Some procedures will work for you and some will not.) If after trying three procedures you have not solved the problem, talk things over with your classroom teacher or a writing center tutor. *You are not expected to try every procedure each time you work through a chapter.*

- If you are not having any problems but want to discover more effective or efficient procedures, read through the book with an eye toward procedures you can try the next time you write. If you try a procedure and like it, use it again. Otherwise, look for something else to try.

As you work to become a better writer with this book as one of your coaches, remember one thing: Following the procedures in this book will not guarantee complete success. These procedures are problem-solving strategies meant to ease the way. No set of procedures can guarantee success, but the ones in this book can help you down the road to your goal.

WORKING
IT
OUT

A Troubleshooting Guide
for Writers

The Big Picture:
An Overview
of the Writing Process
and Essay Structure

Perhaps you think that a "good" writer can produce an effective piece in a minimum amount of time with very little effort. Lots of people believe this notion, but it is far from the truth. On the contrary, successful writers work and rework their pieces carefully through a series of stages, and this process involves considerable time. That is, more than anything else, writing is a process of *rewriting*.

THE WRITING PROCESS

Most successful writers work through a process that involves four primary stages:

1. Prewriting
2. Drafting
3. Revising
4. Editing

Let's look at what each of these stages involves.

1

Prewriting

We should get one thing straight right away: If you sit around waiting for inspiration before you write, you may never get anything written. You see, inspiration does not occur often enough for writers to depend on it. In fact, inspiration occurs so rarely that writers must develop other means for getting their ideas. Collectively, the procedures for coming up with ideas in the absence of inspiration are called *prewriting.* The term *prewriting* is used because these procedures come before writing the first draft.

Chapters 2 and 3 describe procedures for coming up with ideas to write about and for discovering ways to order those ideas. If you follow some of these procedures, you can avoid staring at a blank page waiting for inspiration that may never come.

Drafting

Once writers feel they have generated enough ideas during prewriting to serve as a departure point, they make their first attempt at getting those ideas down. This part of the writing process is *drafting.* Typically, the first draft is very rough, which is why it so often is called the *rough draft.* The rough draft provides raw material that can be shaped and refined in the next stages of the writing process. Chapters 4 through 8 describe procedures you can try when you draft.

Revising

Revising calls on the writer to take the raw material of the draft and rework it to get it in shape for the reader. This reworking is a time-consuming, difficult part of the process. It requires the writer to refine the content so that it is clear, so that points are adequately supported, and so that ideas are expressed in the best way possible and in the best order possible. The procedures described in Chapters 9 through 14 can help you when you revise.

Editing

Experienced readers will expect your writing to be free of errors. Therefore, you have a responsibility to find and eliminate mistakes so that they do not distract or annoy your reader. Many writers make the mistake of hunting for errors too soon, before they have revised for the larger concerns of content and effective expression. Editing should really be saved for the end of the process. When you are ready to edit, the procedures in Chapters 15 through 23 can help you.

Writing Does Not Progress in a Straight Line

Although successful writing progresses in stages, writers do not always move in a straight line from prewriting to drafting to revising to editing. Instead, writers often double back before going forward. For example, while drafting you may think of a new idea to add, so in essence you have left drafting and doubled back to prewriting. While editing you may think of a better way to phrase an idea, so in essence you have left editing and doubled back to revising. Never consider any stage of the process "done" and hence behind you. Always stand ready to go back to an earlier stage when a new idea strikes you.

Developing Your Own Writing Process

Although we have been talking about "the" writing process, there really is no single, correct process. Instead, all writers come to develop procedures that work well for them, so that every successful writer can have a different, successful process. As you use this book and work to become a better writer, try a range of procedures for prewriting, drafting, revising, and editing. Some of these procedures will work well for you and some will not. Incorporate into your writing process those procedures that work well. Continue sampling until you have strategies for handling all the stages of writing, and at that point you will have discovered your own successful process.

THE CONTEXT FOR WRITING

Circumstances influence everything we do—including our writing. Even if you are writing just a grocery list, circumstances such as how much money you have, what the store specials are, what produce is in season, and what you like to eat will influence what you put on your list. Are you doing the shopping, or is a friend doing it for you? If you are the one who must read the list, you might abbreviate heavily and write sloppily, but if someone else must read it, then you probably will abbreviate less and write more legibly. Are you in a hurry? If so, you might arrange your list according to the way the food aisles are set up so you can get in and out quickly. Yes, circumstances influence even the simplest writing task.

Typically, three circumstances influence the writer enough that they form the *context* for writing. These factors are:

1. The writer's purpose

2. The writer's audience

3. The writer's role

The pages that follow will explain these three circumstances. If you need help identifying them for your own writing, see "Identify Your Writing Context" on page 25.

The Writer's Purpose

Even when you write something as basic and simple as a shopping list, you have a purpose for your writing: You want to be sure that you do not forget to buy anything. Similarly, all writing is written for a specific purpose. For example, a letter to a friend may be written to *share* what is happening in the writer's life. The owner's manual for a VCR is written to *inform* the reader of how to operate the device. A newspaper editorial endorsing a political candidate is written to *persuade* readers to vote for that candidate. A short story is written, in part, to *entertain* a reader. Thus, there are four basic purposes for writing:

1. To share

2. To inform

3. To persuade

4. To entertain

Your purpose for writing will affect what you say and how you say it. For example, assume that you plan to write about your first day on a new job. Also assume that your first day was completely miserable. If your purpose is to entertain, you might describe the events of the day in an exaggerated, humorous fashion. However, if your purpose is to share the events with your best friend, who lives 400 miles away, you would probably explain how the events made you feel. If your purpose is to inform your reader of what happened, you would state the events without exaggerating or explaining how they made you feel. Finally, if your purpose is to persuade, you might follow your account of what happened with the argument that new employees need a better orientation program so their first days are not as bad as yours was. Of course, if you want to combine purposes, your detail will be affected accordingly. If you want to entertain your friend while you are sharing your feelings, then you would include humor with your explanation of how you felt.

The Writer's Audience

Your audience (that is, the person or people who will read your writing) is the second element that forms the context for writing. This is because your reader will influence what you say and how you say it. For example, let's say that you need to borrow $100 to get through the month because you did not live within your budget. If you were writing a close friend to request the loan, your writing would be relaxed and informal. You might not even explain why you have come up short or when exactly you will repay the money. Part of your letter might be something like this:

I hate to do this to you, Dale, but I need a hundred bucks fast, never mind why. It's a sad story. I'll get it back to you as soon as I can.

If you were writing to your parents, you would be a little more formal and forthcoming about why you need the money and how you will pay it back:

My phone bill was higher than I expected, so I've come up short this month. I'm really sorry—I've learned my lesson about calling Jan every day. I plan to work overtime three days next week, so I know I can repay the loan after my next paycheck.

How your reader feels about you will also influence your detail and word choice. For example, it may be easier to write a letter to convince your parents, who love you, to loan you $100 than it would be to persuade your boss to advance you the money. In what ways might the detail and word choice for these two letters differ?

Similarly, your detail and word choice will be affected by your reader's situation. For example, assume you are writing to convince your reader that a longer school year is a good idea. If your audience includes working mothers, you might mention that a longer school year will cut down on child-care hassles. However, if your audience includes teenagers, this argument would mean little. Instead, you might note that they would be more competitive when they apply for admission into college.

One way to gear your detail and word choice to your audience is to complete a reader profile to get a sense of your reader's makeup. Such a profile can be like the one on pages 73 through 74.

Perhaps you are thinking that this discussion of audience is meaningless if you are in a writing class because your audience will be your writing instructor. Keep in mind, however, that writing teachers are adept at assuming the identities of different audiences (it is part of their job) so you can write for a range of readers.

The Writer's Role

Each of us plays many roles in life: child, student, ballplayer, sister, brother, spouse, musician, salesclerk, coach, friend, tutor, roommate, and so forth. As a writer, you also play a role, and this role will affect what you write. For example, if your role is that of a student writing for a teacher, then you will be careful to conform to all the terms of the assignment. If you are an employee writing for your boss, then you will work hard to sound polite and competent. If you are writing to someone in your role of a friend, your word choice might be very informal; it may even include slang. However, if you are writing a cover letter in the role of job applicant, then you will try to avoid slang.

Three writing tasks, three contexts.   Assume that you borrowed your roommate's car and that while it was parked someone sideswiped it, causing extensive damage. Now assume you have three writing tasks ahead of you:

1. You must leave your roommate a note explaining what happened to the car.

2. You must write your parents to explain what happened so you can borrow money to have the car fixed.

3. You want to write to your friend who attends another school and tell that person what happened.

How will these three pieces of writing differ? In what ways will the writer's context be responsible for those differences? After considering your answers, compare them with those of some of your classmates.

ESSAY STRUCTURE

Essay structure refers to the way an essay is put together. You already know the most basic fact about essay structure: an essay has a beginning, a middle, and an end.

The Introduction

The beginning is the *introduction,* and its purpose is to stimulate your reader's interest so he or she wants to read on. Sometimes the introduction provides background information your reader may need in order to appreciate the rest of your essay.

In addition to stimulating interest and/or providing background, the introduction often includes the *thesis,* which is the sentence or two that explains what the essay is about. A good thesis presents an idea worth writing about—something that is disputed or in need of explanation:

Acceptable thesis:	Although everyone agrees that children must be adequately cared for, this country does not properly regulate daycare centers.
Explanation:	The thesis idea is open to debate and in need of explanation.
Unacceptable thesis:	Children must be adequately cared for.
Explanation:	No one will disagree with the thesis idea, so why bother writing about it?
Acceptable thesis:	Rose Lewin, my grandmother, is a woman of courage and determination.
Explanation:	The thesis idea is in need of explanation.
Unacceptable thesis:	Rose Lewin is my grandmother.
Explanation:	The thesis idea is a statement of fact that requires no explanation; no one would dispute it.

☞ *Note: For more on the thesis, see page 31.*

Suggestions for ways to handle the introduction appear in Chapter 5. However, to give you an idea of how an introduction can stimulate interest and present the thesis, here is a sample introduction taken from a student essay:

Material to create interest.

Thesis idea: The mortician would be respected more if people understood his or her role.

Go to any elementary school and ask children what they want to be when they grow up, and you will get the usual assortment of answers: police officers, fire fighters, football players, teachers, doctors, and rock stars. You can be sure that not one child will respond, "Mortician." This, of course, is no surprise. It is, however, regrettable. It is regrettable because our society values its safety workers, athletes, teachers, medical professionals, and entertainers, but it cares little for the people who prepare the dead for burial. Yet when death does come to us or a loved one, the mortician will perform a valuable service. Perhaps if we better understood the role of a mortician, we would give this important professional more respect.

The Body Paragraphs

The middle of the essay is formed by the *body paragraphs,* where you present the points that will prove or explain the idea in the thesis. The points you make in the body are often called *supporting details* because they are *details* that *support* the thesis idea.

Supporting details must be *adequate,* which means you must have enough of them to prove or explain the thesis to your reader's satisfaction. In addition, supporting details must be *relevant,* which means they must be clearly related to both the thesis and the focus of the body paragraph. The focus of a particular body paragraph can be presented in a sentence or two known as the *topic sentence.*

The following paragraph was taken from the same student essay from which the sample introduction was taken. Studying it may help you appreciate the structure of a body paragraph.

Topic sentence idea: Focus of paragraph will be the inaccurate image of morticians.

Supporting details are adequate and relevant.

Unfortunately, many people have an image of the mortician that is way off target. They picture a humorless man dressed in a black suit and black top hat. The mortician, they think, delights in death because it means profit. They see the mortician—still thought of as an undertaker—as someone who preys on people's grief and cons them into spending huge sums on caskets and unnecessary services. In short, they see the mortician as unprincipled, as a vulture who feasts on death. Yet morticians are not like this at all. They are pleasant people who desire to help

> others cope with their grief and who see to the
> needs of the departed. Today's morticians dress
> in stylish suits, often gray or blue, and they
> help their clients stay within their budgets,
> not overspend. In fact, various state and fed-
> eral laws prevent morticians from taking finan-
> cial advantage of grief-stricken survivors. Far
> from a ghoul, the mortician is as pleasant and
> full of life as anyone else.

Writers have many strategies for providing adequate detail, including describing, telling a story, giving examples, explaining causes
and/or effects, showing similarities and/or differences, and showing
how something is made or done. As you read, notice the strategies
other writers use. Try them as you work to provide adequate, relevant
detail in your body paragraphs.

☞ *Note: For more on strategies for providing adequate detail, see Chapter 6.*

The Conclusion

The end of an essay is the *conclusion.* You should shape your conclusion carefully because it influences your reader's last impression, and
last impressions are important. To realize this, just think back to the
last movie or television show you watched that had a terrible ending.
Remember how annoyed you were?

Ways to handle conclusions are given in Chapter 7. For now, here is
a sample conclusion, taken from the same student essay that the previous example paragraphs came from.

Conclusion
creates a sense
of closure.
> Morticians are well-educated. They complete
> a strenuous curriculum in a school of mortuary
> science, a curriculum that includes biology,
> anatomy, and related courses. A mortician must
> pass a state examination and serve an apprentice-
> ship before earning a license to practice. Morti-
> cians train hard and serve society in important
> ways. Thus, the modern mortician deserves our
> respect.

A Sample Essay

The sample paragraphs in the preceding sections were taken from the
student essay that follows. As you read this essay, pay particular attention to structure.

THE MODERN MORTICIAN

Material to create interest.

Go to any elementary school and ask children what they want to be when they grow up, and you will get the usual assortment of answers: police officers, fire fighters, football players, teachers, doctors, and rock stars. You can be sure that not one child will respond, "Mortician." This, of course, is no surprise. It is, however, regrettable. It is regrettable because our society values its safety workers, athletes, teachers, medical professionals, and entertainers, but it cares little for the people who prepare the dead for burial. Yet when death does come to us or a loved one, the mortician will perform a valuable service. Perhaps if we better understood the role of a mortician, we would give this important professional more respect.

Thesis idea: The mortician would be respected more if people understood his or her role.

Topic sentence idea: Focus of paragraph will be the inaccurate image of morticians.

Unfortunately, many people have an image of the mortician that is way off target. They picture a humorless man dressed in a black suit and black top hat. The mortician, they think, delights in death because it means profit. They see the mortician—still thought of as an undertaker—as someone who preys on people's grief and cons them into spending huge sums on caskets and unnecessary services. In short, they see the mortician as unprincipled, as a vulture who feasts on death. Yet morticians are not like this at all. They are pleasant people who desire to help others cope with their grief and who see to the needs of the departed. Today's morticians dress in stylish suits, often gray or blue, and they help their clients stay within their budgets, not overspend. In fact, various state and federal laws prevent morticians from taking financial advantage of grief-stricken survivors. Far from a ghoul, the mortician is as pleasant and full of life as anyone else.

Supporting details are adequate and relevant.

Topic sentence idea: Morticians prepare bodies for burial.

The primary responsibility of morticians is preparing the body for burial. They drain the blood and other fluids and inject a preservative. They give the body as lifelike

Supporting details are adequate and relevant.

a representation as possible, and in the case of accident or extended illness, they often perform what seem like miracles to give the deceased a natural, peaceful appearance that comforts the mourners. The process of preparing the body also protects society from disease. If bodies were not disposed of properly, their decay would lead to widespread infection. Furthermore, morticians are trained to recognize a variety of serious contagious diseases and report signs of them to public health officials.

Topic sentence idea: Morticians help with funeral arrangements.

At a time when family members are experiencing a great deal of grief, the mortician steps in to help with funeral arrangements. To relieve the burden on the family, the mortician secures the permit for burial, makes arrangements with the clergy, and notifies the newspaper. The mortician discusses all options with the family and helps them make decisions they are comfortable with. When a family has no strong religious affiliation, the mortician may even fulfill some of the functions of the clergy, such as suggesting whether to have calling hours and when and where to have them, what kind of service is appropriate, and where the burial will take place. In addition, the mortician can provide a chapel for those who desire one.

Supporting details are adequate and relevant.

Topic sentence idea: The mortician counsels the grieving.

It is not uncommon for a mortician to counsel those who are unable to cope with the death of a loved one. Although not a trained psychologist, the mortician is so familiar with the grief and stress that accompany death that he or she can offer the words, sympathetic ear, and kind touch the grieving need. A mortician who cannot provide adequate help is quick to make a referral to the proper mental health agency.

Supporting details are adequate and relevant.

Conclusion creates a sense of closure.

Morticians are well-educated. They complete a strenuous curriculum in a school of mortuary science, a curriculum that includes biology, anatomy, and related courses. A mortician must pass a state examination and serve an apprenticeship before earning a license to

> practice. Morticians train hard and serve soci-
> ety in important ways. Thus, the modern morti-
> cian deserves our respect.

HOW TO BECOME A BETTER WRITER

Becoming a better writer has much in common with becoming a better swimmer, becoming a better piano player, or becoming a better basketball player. In all these cases, a person is working to improve a skill. As you work to improve your writing skills, keep the following suggestions in mind.

1. **Be patient.** Improving a skill takes time, and just as perfecting a foul shot takes a basketball player considerable time and practice, so too will improving your writing. If you expect too much too soon, you will become frustrated. So set reasonable goals for yourself by looking for slow, steady progress rather than dramatic, overnight improvement.

2. **Expect to get stuck.** Everyone does, even experienced, professional writers. Writer's block and dead ends are all part of writing, so do not think there is something wrong with you if you have some trouble. Consult this text, your instructor, other experienced writers, and/or a writing center tutor when you get stuck. When you solve the problem, tuck the solution away for future reference, so the same problem does not plague you over and over again.

3. **Remember that writing is really rewriting.** Experienced writers work and rework drafts a number of times before they are satisfied. With each revision, you will learn a little more about writing, so welcome rewrites as learning opportunities, and know that you are acting like an experienced writer each time you revise.

4. **Be aware of what you do when you write.** Decide which procedures work well for you and which ones do not. Then consult this text and your instructor for procedures to replace the ones that did not work. For example, maybe idea generation goes well for you, but revision does not. That means you need to discover new revision procedures. When your procedures work better, your writing will improve.

5. **Talk to other writers.** Find out what they do when they write, and try out some of their procedures to see if they work for you. When you need ideas, talk to others and kick around possibilities. Share your frustrations and successes. Form a network with your class-mates and other writers for support and suggestions. You can help each other improve.

6. **Study the responses to your writing.** What does your instructor say about your writing? What do your classmates say when they read your drafts? What do people in the writing center say? Reader re-sponse is invaluable to a writer. By paying attention to this response and working to improve areas where readers see weaknesses, you can improve more quickly. If you do not understand a response made by your instructor or another reader, or if you do not know how to make a change, be sure to ask for help.

7. **Read, read, read.** Read every day—the newspaper, your textbooks, newsmagazines, short stories, novels. Read anything that interests you. As you read, pay attention to how other writers handle intro-ductions, conclusions, supporting detail, and transitions. Look up unfamiliar words, notice sentence structure, and observe punctua-tion. Try to incorporate strategies that you observe in your reading into some of your writing. The more you read, the more you will in-ternalize about the nature of our language, and the faster your writ-ing will improve. Furthermore, frequent reading will make you more knowledgeable, so you will have more ideas to include in your writing.

8. **Do not be afraid of mistakes.** They are a natural part of learning. Go ahead and give your writing your best shot. Take some risks; try some things out. If you make mistakes, embrace them—use them as opportunities to learn. If you are afraid of making a mistake, you will never try; if you never try, you will never grow.

MYTHS ABOUT WRITING

People believe many things about writing—and much of what they be-lieve is not true. Following is a list of some commonly believed myths about writing. If you are surprised to learn that certain of the "facts" listed are untrue, be sure to check the chapter indicated for the accu-rate information.

Myth	Accurate Information
Writers are born, not made.	Preface
"Good" writers rarely struggle.	Chapter 1
Writers should wait for inspiration.	Chapter 2
"Good" writers get it right the first time.	Chapters 4–14
"Good" writers write fast.	Chapters 9–14
Outlining is very time-consuming.	Chapter 3
Introductions should be written first.	Chapter 5
The best conclusions summarize the main points.	Chapter 7
The longer the words, the better they are.	Chapter 8
The longer the writing, the better it is.	Chapter 12
Revising involves reading over a draft and fixing spelling and punctuation.	Chapter 10
Only English teachers understand grammar rules.	Chapters 15–23
Sentence fragments are always short.	Chapter 16
Run-ons and comma splices are always long.	Chapter 17
Use a comma wherever you pause in speech.	Chapter 21
There are no rules to explain English spelling.	Chapter 23

PART 1

Prewriting

Before you begin drafting, you should lay some groundwork by discovering something about what you want to say and the order you can say it in. This groundwork is known as prewriting. *Without prewriting, you can find yourself staring for prolonged periods at a blank page. Or you can find yourself beginning, wadding up the paper, beginning again, wadding up more paper, and on and on. The chapters in this section can help you avoid this kind of frustration and waste of time. They describe strategies for coming up with ideas you can write about and ways to order those ideas.*

CHAPTER

2

"I Don't Know
What to Write."

THE TERROR OF THE BLANK PAGE! No, it's not a movie coming
soon to a theater near you. It's the fear writers experience when they
sit down to write and cannot think of anything to say. Sure, sometimes
writers are zapped by the lightning bolt of inspiration, and idea after
idea comes tumbling forth. However, inspiration is fickle and cannot
be counted on to show up just because you have a writing project due
a week from Friday. Therefore, if inspiration fails you, you must take
steps to develop writing ideas on your own. The following strategies,
known as *idea generation techniques,* can help you come up with ideas
when inspiration does not arrive on time.

TRY FREEWRITING

The act of writing stimulates thought, so when you cannot think of
anything to write, start writing anyway. Eventually, ideas will surface.

Freewriting is an idea generation technique that lets you use writing
to discover ideas to write about. It works like this: Sit in a quiet spot
and write nonstop for about ten minutes. Record every idea that occurs

to you, no matter how silly or irrelevant it may seem. Do not stop for any reason; just keep your pen moving. If you run out of ideas, write the days of the week, names of your family members, even "I don't know what to write." Write *anything*. Soon new thoughts will strike you, and you can write about them.

The important thing about freewriting is to be *free,* so make wild statements, write silly notions, or make random associations. Do not evaluate the worth of anything; if it occurs to you, write it down. Do not worry about grammar, spelling, punctuation, or neatness—just write ideas the best way you can without worrying over anything.

Here is a freewriting produced to discover ideas for an essay about the effects of computers:

> *Computers are wonderful and scarry at the same time. They are great because they make things easier and faster, like writing things and getting info. Lets see, what else? They store info and trade it with other computers so our privacy can be invaded, that's pretty scarry. Lap top computers are big now, you see people use them everywhere. That's good and bad because you can work when its convenient but you also work when you should be resting. This whole Internet thing is wierd. People spend whole days on it. Is that productive or lost time? What else? 1 2 3 4 5 6 7 8 Pornography is a problem on the Internet and kids can get involved. Yuk. Now what else? I'm stuck, I'm stuck. If you don't understand computers, you will have trouble in the job market. I guess that means schools better do a good job of teaching this stuff. Now what? Anything else? Expensive. Who can afford all this computer equipment? Is it just for the rich? I read an articel that said computers are changing the way we communicate. I don't remember what all it said, I should look it up. I think I'm out of ideas, I'm quiting.*

Note that the freewriting unearthed a number of ideas for an essay about the effects of computers: convenience, possible invasion of privacy, changes in the way people work, the time spent on the Internet, changes in the way people communicate, the need for schools to educate children in computer skills, whether or not computer access is just for the rich. Obviously, these are too many points for one essay, so the writer would narrow things down to one topic—perhaps changes in the way people communicate or the advantages and disadvantages of the Internet.

TRY CLUSTERING

Clustering is a powerful idea generation technique because it lets you see at a glance how ideas relate to one another. To cluster, write in the middle of a page a subject area you want to think about. Then draw a circle around the subject, so you have something that looks like this:

drug abuse

Next, as you think of ideas, connect them to the central circle to get something like this:

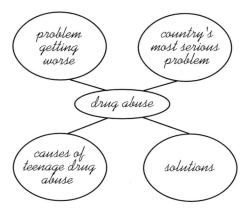

As more ideas occur to you, connect them to the appropriate circles (the ones with ideas the new ideas are most closely related to) to get something like this:

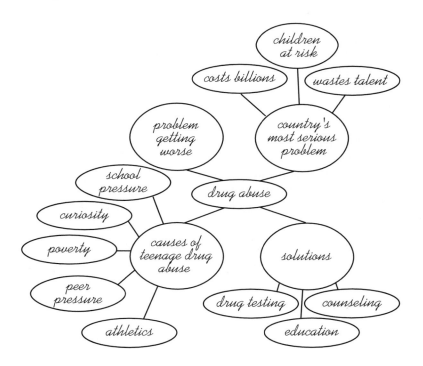

Continue writing ideas and joining them to circles until you can think of nothing else. When you can think of nothing else, study your clustering to see if one particular circle with its connecting circles gives you enough to begin a draft. For example, this portion of the previous clustering might serve as a departure point for a draft about causes of teenage drug abuse:

If this clustering does not yield enough ideas for a draft, try yet another clustering to expand the branches:

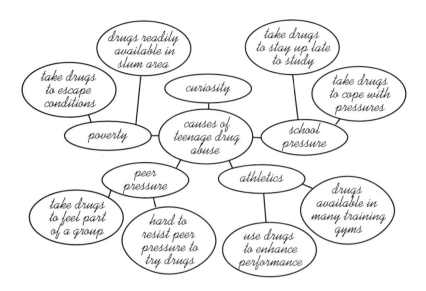

TRY LISTING

An idea generation list looks just like a shopping list: It is a vertical listing of things that occur to you, written in phrases rather than sentences. To be successful at listing, you must not censor yourself; write down everything you think of. Even if you are sure an idea is perfectly rotten, get it down anyway because it may prompt you to think of another, more worthy idea. Here is an idea generation list for an essay about the effects of being cut from the freshman basketball team:

> *felt rejected*
> *was embarrassed*
> *disappointed my father*
> *got teased*
> *felt inadequate*
> *gave up basketball forever*
> *decided to go out for cross-country*
> *lost my best friend, who was busy*
>   *with the team*

After listing, look over what you have and cross out ideas you do not want to use and/or add new ideas that occur to you. A benefit of listing is that by numbering the ideas in the list in the order you want to treat them in your draft, you can easily develop a scratch outline.

Sometimes you may wish to write a second list focusing on only one of the points in your first list. For example, a second list focusing on "lost my best friend, who was busy with the team" could look like this:

Cal had no time for me
practiced every day
couldn't go out at night because of curfew
socialized with his teammates
wouldn't play sports with me because of fear of injuries

TRY BRAINSTORMING

To brainstorm for ideas to write about, ask yourself questions about your topic. The answers can provide details for your essay. Sometimes the question that offers up the most is the simple question "Why?" In addition, you may find the following questions helpful:

Why did it happen?	What is it different from?
How did it happen?	What are its physical
Who was involved?	characteristics?
When did it happen?	Why is it important?
Where did it happen?	Who would care about it?
Could it happen again?	What causes it?
What does it mean?	What are its effects?
How does it work?	What is it related to?
Why does this matter to me?	What examples are there?
Why does this matter to my reader?	How can it be explained?
Why is it true?	What controversies are
What is it similar to?	associated with it?

EXAMINE YOUR TOPIC
FROM DIFFERENT ANGLES

If you have a broad subject area you want to write about, but you are not sure how to approach or limit the subject, try viewing it from different angles. Asking yourself the following questions can help you see how to approach your topic from different perspectives:

1. **How can I describe my subject?** What does it look, smell, taste, sound, and feel like? What are its parts, its color, its size, its shape, and so on?

2. **How can I compare and contrast my subject?** What is it like, and what is it different from? Are the similarities and differences important?

3. **What do I associate my subject with?** What does it make me or others think of? What is it related to? What does it develop from or lead to?

4. **How can I analyze my subject?** How is it broken down? How does it work? What is it made of? Why is it important? Is it part of something bigger?

5. **How can I apply my subject?** What is it good for? Who would find it useful? When is it useful? Does it have social, economic, or political value?

6. **What arguments accompany my subject?** What are the reasons for it? What are the reasons against it? Who is for it? Who is against it?

After answering these questions, you may have an approach to your subject—analysis, comparison, argument, or whatever. Then you can do some additional idea generation to develop ideas to suit your approach.

WRITE AN EXPLORATORY DRAFT

Sometimes when you do not know what to write, the solution is to get in there and start writing anyway. You may be one of those people who don't know what they want to say until they say it. If so, sit down and force yourself to write on your topic for about an hour without worrying about how good the material is. The result will be an exploratory draft, a few pages of material reflecting your current thinking. An exploratory draft may yield a thought or two that you can pursue with one or more of the idea generation techniques in this chapter, or it may yield enough for you to try an outline or rough draft. If you write an exploratory draft, remember that your goal is not to produce a first draft of your essay; it is to discover one or more ideas to serve as a departure point.

RELATE THE TOPIC TO YOUR OWN EXPERIENCE

When you are assigned a topic, and ideas do not occur to you, try relating the topic to your own experiences and observations. For example, if you have been asked to write about modern technology, remember all the trouble your used car has caused you, and write an essay about how cars can be more trouble than they are worth. Or recall all the times computer errors have caused you problems and write about the frustrations of the computer age. If you have been asked to write about the American educational system, you might remember the hearing-impaired student you graduated from high school with and decide to describe how we fail to meet the needs of special students. Or perhaps you will consider your college experience and argue that too much emphasis is placed on athletics. A topic that seems formidable at first can be cut down to size and made manageable if it is viewed in the context of your own life and past experiences.

TALK INTO A TAPE RECORDER

If the writing techniques in this chapter do not help you come up with ideas, forget writing for a while and try talking. Have a conversation with yourself about your topic by speaking all your thoughts into a tape recorder. Do not censor yourself; just talk about whatever occurs to you, and feel free to be silly, offbeat, funny, dramatic, or outlandish. When you run out of ideas, play back the tape. When you hear an idea that could find its way into your writing, pause the tape and write the idea down.

TALK TO OTHER PEOPLE

Discuss your writing topic with your friends and relatives. They may be able to suggest ideas to include in your writing. Or have other people ask you questions about your topic. Your answers may include ideas you can use to develop your topic. The brainstorming questions on page 22 can provide a starting point.

PUT YOUR TOPIC ON THE BACK BURNER

If you do not know what to write, you may need to give your ideas an incubation period. Try going about your normal routine with your writing topic on the back burner. Think about your topic from time to time throughout the day. Many writers report that they get some of their best ideas while walking the dog, washing the car, sitting in a traffic jam, cleaning the house, and such. If you are feeling anxious, exercise to help relieve the tension. Of course, if an idea strikes you while you are in the middle of something, be sure to stop and write the idea down so you do not forget it.

IDENTIFY YOUR WRITING CONTEXT

You may have trouble thinking of ideas if you have not clarified your purpose, audience, and role (the writing context; see page 3). Responding to the following can help.

1. **To identify your purpose:**

   a. What feelings, ideas, or experiences can I share with my reader?

   b. Of what can I inform my reader?

   c. Of what can I persuade my reader?

   d. In what way can I entertain my reader?

2. **To identify your audience:**

   a. Who could learn something from my writing?

   b. Who would enjoy reading about my topic?

   c. Who could be influenced to think or act a certain way?

   d. Who is interested in my topic or would find it important?

   e. Who needs to hear what I have to say?

3. **If you have trouble establishing your role, try one of these:**

student	citizen	friend	child
employee	neutral party	authority	spouse
parent	average,	woman or man	
teenager	general reader	consumer	

KEEP A JOURNAL

Buy a full-size spiral notebook for keeping a journal, and write in it every day. A journal is not a diary because it is not a record of your daily activities. Instead, it is an account of your thoughts and reactions to events in your life. For example, if you feel compassion for a blind person you saw, describe your feelings. If you are anxious about an upcoming event, explain why you are concerned. If you were recently reminded of the time you realized that your parents were not perfect, describe this memory.

In addition to recording your reaction to events, a journal is a good place to think things through in writing. Is something troubling you? Do you have a problem? Explore the issues in your journal, and you may achieve new insights. In addition, if you are working on a writing project, a journal is an ideal place to try some idea generation, try out an approach to part of the draft, or tinker with a revision. A journal is also an excellent place to respond to what goes on in your classes. Use it to summarize class notes, to respond to reading assignments, and to react to lectures. Journal activities like these will help you learn course material. Later, if you are looking for a writing topic, review your journal for ideas.

Because your journal is meant for you and not for a reader, you do not need to revise and edit anything. Just get your ideas down any way that suits you because you are your primary audience this time.

The best way to handle journal writing is to set aside at least fifteen minutes at the same time every day to write. If you have trouble thinking of what to write, try one of the following suggestions:

1. Write about something that angers you, that pleases you, or that frustrates you.

2. Write about a problem you have.

3. Write about some change you would like to make in yourself.

4. Write about your goals.

5. Write about someone you admire.

6. Describe your life as you would like it to be in five years.

7. Describe your favorite teacher or your best friend.

8. Record a vivid childhood memory.

9. Describe the best and worst features of your school.

10. Describe your current writing process, including what you do to generate ideas, draft, revise, and edit.

11. Freewrite, beginning with the first thought that comes to mind.

12. Record your reactions to your writing class so far: What do you find confusing? What has been helpful? What topics would you like to cover? What do you think of the pace of instruction? What else would you like the instructor to know so he or she can better meet your needs?

COMBINE TECHNIQUES

No law states "Only one idea generation technique per customer," so feel free to combine techniques any way you like. Perhaps you will begin with freewriting and then try brainstorming. Or maybe you will talk into a tape recorder and then list. Experiment until you find the combination of techniques that works the best for you.

DEVELOP YOUR OWN WRITING TOPIC

If you must come up with your own writing topic, some of the following strategies may help.

1. Try freewriting (see page 17). Begin your freewriting something like this: "I need a writing topic. Let's see, maybe I could write about . . ."

2. Try clustering (see page 19). Begin by placing one of these subjects in a circle in the center of the page: education, athletics, friendship, television, movies, family relationships, automobiles, teenagers, memories, technology, the environment. After clustering for a while, try a second clustering with one of the circles from the previous clustering at the center. Continue in this way until you have a topic.

3. Skim magazines and newspapers for ideas. An article on the movie-rating system could prompt you to write that we need to change the current rating system, or an article on the Olympics could prompt you to write that the government should subsidize athletes.

4. Consult your journal for topic ideas (see page 25).

5. Fill in the blanks in the following sentences to arrive at possible writing topics:

   a. I'll never forget the time I _____.

b. The best thing about _____ is _____.

c. The worst thing about _____ is _____.

d. My most embarrassing moment occurred when _____.

e. My proudest moment occurred when _____.

f. I wish I could change _____.

g. After _____ I changed my mind about _____.

h. _____ is the most unforgettable person I know.

i. _____ is the most _____ I know.

j. The best way to _____ is _____.

k. Few people understand the true meaning of _____.

l. What this country needs is _____.

m. Without _____, life would be very different.

n. _____ made a lasting impression on me.

o. Few people understand the differences between ____ and ____.

p. _____ and _____ are more alike than people realize.

Filling in the blanks in these sentences will not give you ready-to-use topics, but the completed sentences will *suggest* topics. For example, consider this completed sentence:

```
I wish I could change the way public education is funded
in this state.
```

This sentence could lead to the following topic:

```
Rather than using the property tax, this state should fi-
nance public education with an increased income tax.
```

6. Make a list of questions or problems, and use one of the questions or problems as a departure point for additional idea generation. For example, your list could include some of the following:

a. Do nice people really finish last?

b. What is the best way to find a job?

c. How can I lose ten pounds quickly and safely?

d. Why do women wear makeup when men don't?

e. How can I improve my conversation skills?

f. Is it too late to save our environment?

g. Why do so few people vote?

h. Why are violent movies so popular?

When you can think of no more questions or problems, pick one from your list to be the focus of additional idea generation.

USE A COMPUTER

If you use a computer, you may like the following strategies.

Freewriting

A computer is great for freewriting. (See page 17 for an explanation of freewriting.) With a full, blank screen, begin to write whatever comes to mind about your subject (or even your lack of a subject). Do not go back with the delete key, the backspace key, or even the left arrow key. Just write for about five or ten minutes. Then get a printout, so you can read what you have typed.

Underline useable ideas. Perhaps there will be enough to get you started. If not, do a second freewriting focusing on the underlined ideas.

Blindfolded Writing

Let's say you have tried freewriting, but you don't feel free because you cannot resist going back to reread what you have written, check for errors, and think what to say next. A strategy that can help with your problem is writing blindfolded. No, you don't really blindfold yourself or even close your eyes. Just find the switch that controls the brightness of the monitor and turn it all the way down until the screen is dark. Then type for five to ten minutes, just as you would if you were freewriting. When you are done, your screen may look like this:

```
I kdon;t know what to write I think I;ll write about the
problems of students are getting wripped off on the fees
and tuition being changerd.
```

That's no problem. You can still detect the seeds of good ideas to expand on in a draft or in a second blindfolded writing.

Listing and Writing a Scratch Outline

Listing, a popular idea generation technique, is described on page 2. Although many writers like listing, some people claim it is too messy for them because of all the crossing out, arrow drawing, and inserting that can be involved. If you are among this latter group, you may appreciate listing on the computer because ideas can be easily reorganized and deleted to get a neat, sequenced list of ideas.

To list at the computer, write the first idea that comes to mind. A word or a phrase will do just fine. Press the enter or return key. Write another idea, and press the enter or return key. Repeat these steps until you run out of ideas.

Use your delete key(s) to eliminate ideas you want to strike from your list. Next, study your list and decide what order is suggested. Try out the order using the copy-move sequence that is part of your word processing program. Rearrange your list as often as you like until you have a suitable scratch outline to guide your first draft.

"My Ideas Are All Mixed Up."

Okay, so you've come up with good ideas, you've written them in a draft, and you're feeling confident—until you read over your draft and discover that your ideas do not seem connected to each other. Everything is a jumble. Does this mean your ideas are no good? Absolutely not. Instead, it means you need an organizational framework to help your ideas hang together in a coherent whole. The strategies in this chapter can help you put that framework together.

CHECK YOUR THESIS

Your thesis is the sentence or two that tells what your essay is about. It can be written out (often appearing in the introduction) or strongly suggested by the details in the essay. For more on the thesis, see page 7.

If your ideas seem jumbled, the problem may be with your thesis. Check your thesis against the guidelines that follow and make any adjustments that are necessary.

1. *Be sure you have a thesis.* Can you point to or write out a specific sentence or two that expresses the focus of your writing? If not, your ideas may be merely a collection of loosely related thoughts that seem confused because they do not hang together to develop one central focus.

2. *Be sure your thesis expresses an idea worthy of discussion,* something that is disputed or something in need of explanation. Otherwise, you will be forced into detail that ranges far afield and creates a sense of jumble. For more on this point, see page 7.

3. *Be sure your thesis does not take in too much territory,* or you will be forced to bring in too many ideas, which can create disorder.

Thesis covering too much territory:	High school was a traumatic experience for me.
Acceptable thesis:	My first high school track meet was a traumatic experience for me.
Explanation:	The first thesis requires the writer to cover events spanning four years—a great deal for one essay. The second thesis sets up a more reasonable goal—covering the events of one afternoon.

USE TOPIC SENTENCES

A *topic sentence* presents the main idea of a paragraph. All the details in a paragraph must relate clearly and directly to that topic sentence (see page 8). If your ideas seem mixed up, check to be sure you are using topic sentences to focus your body paragraphs. If you are not, add them. Then compare every sentence in each body paragraph against its topic sentence to be sure that everything relates to that topic sentence. If something does not relate directly, it must be stricken or moved to another paragraph.

WRITE A SCRATCH OUTLINE

To write a scratch outline, list all your main points. Then review the list and number the points in the order you will handle them in your writing. A scratch outline can be made quickly, and many writers find it is all they need to get organized. (For more on the scratch outline, see page 00.) However, because the outline is not very detailed (it covers only the main points), other writers find it does not provide enough structure. If you are one of the latter, you may prefer one of the other outlining techniques described in this chapter.

CONSTRUCT AN OUTLINE TREE

Many writers like the outline tree because it provides a visual representation of how ideas relate to each other. To construct a tree, write your thesis idea on the page:

A refundable deposit should be added to the price of products in glass containers.

Next, branch your main ideas off from your thesis idea:

A refundable deposit should be added to the price of products in glass containers.

| *to reduce litter* | *because voluntary recycling is not working* | *to keep prices down* |

Then, branch supporting ideas off from your main ideas:

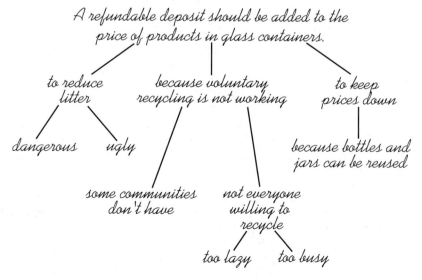

A refundable deposit should be added to the price of products in glass containers.

to reduce litter — *because voluntary recycling is not working* — *to keep prices down*

dangerous — *ugly*

some communities don't have — *not everyone willing to recycle*

because bottles and jars can be reused

too lazy — *too busy*

The value of the outline tree is that it allows you to see at a glance how ideas relate to each other so that when drafting, you avoid skipping randomly from one idea to another.

COMPLETE AN OUTLINE WORKSHEET

An outline worksheet allows you to plan your draft in a fair amount of detail without bothering with the roman numerals, letters, and numbers of a formal outline. To use the worksheet, make a copy of the form in Figure 1 and fill in the blanks with words and phrases that indicate the points you will make in the draft. Then write the draft using the worksheet as a guide.

MAKE OUTLINE CARDS

After you have generated ideas, get a stack of index cards. Write each of your ideas on its own index card, and then arrange the cards in the order you will treat the ideas in your draft. If this order does not work, rearrange the cards and try again.

CONSTRUCT AN OUTLINE MAP

An outline map is a good way to plan a draft and get a visual representation of it. To develop the map, use your list of generated ideas to fill in a copy of the form shown in Figure 2.

To complete the map, write in your preliminary thesis and place one main point at the top of each column. (If you have two main points, you will have two columns; three main points will mean three columns, and so on.) In the columns under each main point, write the supporting ideas that will develop the main point. Then note what your concluding point(s) will be.

The beauty of the outline map is that before you even begin drafting you can check the relevance of ideas by checking what is in each column against the main point at the top, and you can check the relevance of each main point by comparing it to the preliminary thesis. Also, if ideas need to be added or moved around, you can do so relatively easily.

Figure 1
OUTLINE WORKSHEET

Paragraph I

1. Opening comments to stimulate reader's interest:_____

_____

_____

2. Preliminary thesis statement:_____

_____

_____

Paragraph II

1. Main point (topic sentence idea):_____

_____

_____

2. Supporting details to develop main point:_____

_____

_____

_____

Paragraph III

1. Main point (topic sentence idea):_____

_____

_____

2. Supporting details to develop main point:_____

_____

_____

_____

Note: Continue in this way until all main points are treated.

Final paragraph
Ideas to bring writing to closure:_____

_____

_____

Figure 2
OUTLINE MAP

Preliminary thesis: _____

_____

Main Point (Topic Sentence Idea)	Main Point (Topic Sentence Idea)	Main Point (Topic Sentence Idea)	Main Point (Topic Sentence Idea)
Supporting Detail	Supporting Detail	Supporting Detail	Supporting Detail

Concluding points: _____

_____

_____

_____

You can write your draft from the map by allowing each column to be a body paragraph, with each main point expressed in a topic sentence.

WRITE AN ABSTRACT

An *abstract* is a very brief summary. Before you draft, write a one-paragraph abstract of what you plan to say in your writing. Include only the main points, and leave out the details that will expand on those points. Then read over your abstract to check that the main points follow logically one to the next. If they do not, try another abstract, placing your ideas in a different order. When you draft, you can flesh out the abstract into a full-length piece of writing.

WRITE A POSTDRAFT OUTLINE

Some writers prefer to outline their draft *after* it is written to check the organization. To do this, fill in an outline map, outline tree, outline worksheet, or formal outline with the ideas already written in the draft. If you discover points that do not fit logically into a particular section of the outline, you have found an organization problem that needs your attention.

USE TRANSITIONS

Transitions are words and phrases that show how ideas relate to each other. Sometimes when your ideas seem mixed up, you just need to supply appropriate transitions to demonstrate the connections between points. Consider, for example, these sentences:

```
Today's economy is not good for the stock market. There is
still money to be made in speculative stocks.
```

Without a transitional word or phrase, the reader can have a difficult time seeing how the ideas in the two sentences relate to each other. Add a transition, however, and this problem is solved:

```
Today's economy is not good for the stock market. Never-
theless, there is still money to be made in speculative
stocks.
```

The following transitions can help you demonstrate how your ideas relate to each other:

---

also	later	however	in like
and	earlier	on the	fashion
in addition	at the same time	contrary	consequently
furthermore	for example	on the other	as a result
moreover	for instance	hand	therefore
indeed	in other words	yet	nevertheless
in fact	in short	although	for this
in summary	near	even though	reason
in conclusion	in front of	in the same	
now	next to	way	
then	thus	similarly	

Repeat Key Words

You can often demonstrate how ideas relate to each other by repeating a key word or words, like this:

```
The senate is scheduled to vote on the tax reform bill
Wednesday. This bill will reduce taxes.
```

Repeat Key Ideas

You can also demonstrate how ideas relate to each other by repeating a key idea, like this:

```
The senate is scheduled to vote on the tax reform bill
Wednesday. This legislation will reduce taxes.
```

USE A COMPUTER

Computers can be very handy for helping writers organize their ideas. Consider trying the techniques that follow if it seems to you that your ideas are mixed up.

The Scratch Outline

If you use a computer to generate ideas by listing, your list can be turned into a scratch outline very easily. Using the delete key or block erase, eliminate the ideas in your list that you do not want to use (and if new ideas occur to you, add them to the list). Then using the copy-move command for your word processing program, arrange the ideas in your list in the order you want to treat them in your writing.

The Outline Program

If an outline program is available to you, use it to fill in the various levels designated by roman numerals, letters, and numbers. Study the results and expand and delete sublevels as necessary.

The Postdraft Outline

After writing your draft, save the file. Then create a second copy of the draft by renaming the file with an ".OUT" (for *outline*) extension. For example, the file TERMPAPR.DOC would be renamed TERMPAPR.OUT. Reduce this second copy to an outline by identifying in each paragraph the sentence that states the major idea (the topic sentence) and the major supporting details; strip everything else from each paragraph (using the delete key or a block erase), leaving just the sentences that give the main ideas and major supporting details.

Next, identify your thesis sentence and write it at the top of your outline. Now use roman and arabic numbers, capital and lowercase letters to sequence the sentences following the thesis sentence into a formal outline. Study this outline and make any necessary adjustments.

Once the outline is made and adjusted, it can be placed in a window and the original draft can be recalled and revised according to the insights gained from making the outline. If your word processing program does not offer a window, simply print the outline and use it as a revision guide.

Drafting

Drafting *is your first attempt to get your ideas down on the page. Be-cause drafting occurs so early in the writing process, the draft is likely to be very rough. This is normal, so do not feel discouraged if your draft needs considerable work.*

CHAPTER

4

"I Know What I Want to Say, But I Can't Say It."

Okay, so you think you know what you want to say, and you sit down with plenty of fresh writing paper, pencils sharpened to a lethal point, and a bowl of Doritos (so you don't have to break your concentration by heading to the kitchen if you get the munchies in the middle of a paragraph). Then disaster strikes: You know what you want to say, but the words don't come out right—or they don't come out at all.

If this happens to you, be assured that you are not alone. Plenty of writers experience this kind of block. The key to getting past the block to some productive writing rests in trying one or more of the techniques described in this chapter.

GET RID OF DISTRACTIONS

Be honest. Are you trying to write with your headphones on? With MTV in the background? With your roommate rummaging around looking for a missing left sneaker? With the street department outside tearing up the pavement with an air hammer? Few people can write when visual or auditory distractions disrupt their focus, so getting past writer's block may be as simple as finding a place to write that is free of distractions.

WRITE IN A NEW PLACE

Sometimes a change of scene can help a writer break through a block, so if you usually write in one place, try another. Go to the library, the park, or a local diner. If you write in your room, try the lounge or a classroom, or the dining hall. A new locale can give you a fresh perspective.

SWITCH YOUR WRITING TOOLS

If you write with a pen, try a pencil or a typewriter. If you use a typewriter, try a word processor or a pen. If you like lined paper, try unlined. If you like legal pads, try stationery. Do anything to make the writing *feel* different, and you may break through the block.

WRITE ON A DAILY SCHEDULE

Professional writers are usually very disciplined about their work. They make themselves sit down at the same time each day to write for a specific number of hours. You can follow the lead of the professionals by forcing yourself to write at a certain time each day for a specific length of time. This kind of schedule can push you past the block.

WRITE A LETTER TO A FRIEND

Sometimes we become blocked because we tense up. We think of the reader at the other end sitting in judgment of our work, and we freeze. To relax and break the block, write your draft as if it were a letter to a friend—a letter to someone who cares about you and who will continue to value you regardless of how well you write. When your audience is shifted to a person you feel comfortable with, you can relax and allow the words to emerge. After writing a draft this way, you will likely have to revise your work to make it suitable for your intended reader and to shape it into essay or other appropriate forms, but you should have considerable raw material to work with.

WRITE IN A NATURAL STYLE

Sometimes writers try so hard to achieve a "sophisticated" style that the strain causes a block. To solve this problem, write your draft the way you normally speak, and the words should flow more easily. After drafting this way, revise if the writing is too conversational or informal.

SPEAK INTO A TAPE RECORDER

A variation of the previous technique is to speak your draft into a tape recorder. Sometimes we have trouble writing, but we do not have trouble talking. After speaking into a tape recorder, you can transcribe the tape to get your draft.

WRITE FOR YOURSELF INSTEAD OF FOR A READER

Some writers block because they are too focused on the ultimate reader of their writing. They imagine the reader passing judgment, and they become tense. One good solution is to forget your reader for a while and just write the draft in a way that pleases *you.* Be your own audience at first. Later when you polish your work, you can make the changes necessary for the audience you are aiming for.

WALK AWAY

When the words won't come, you may need some time away to relax and let things simmer. Take a walk, listen to music, play tennis, walk the dog, take a shower, make a tuna fish sandwich, read a magazine, clean a drawer, call your mother, or pot a plant. Do anything to clear your mind for a while. Time away can serve as an incubation period, so when you start to write again you are no longer stuck.

SET INTERMEDIATE GOALS FOR YOURSELF

At the beginning of a writing project, the finish line can seem so far away that the task makes us fearful. This fear can lead to writer's block. In this case, the key to getting unstuck is to break the task down into manageable steps. Let the completion of each step be a goal that earns its own reward. For example, the first time you sit down, tell yourself you will just come up with five ideas and a scratch outline. The second time, you will just write the draft of the introduction. The third time, you will draft two more paragraphs. If you work toward the completion of intermediate goals, the project will be less intimidating.

WRITE THE INTRODUCTION LAST

No one ever said a writer had to start at the beginning. If you cannot get the introduction down, write the rest of your essay and then go back to it. With the rest of your draft complete, you may find your introduction easier to handle than it was when you attempted it before. (If you write your introduction last, write a preliminary thesis on scratch paper early in the process so you have a focus for your draft.)

CONCENTRATE ON WHAT YOU <u>CAN</u> DO AND SKIP WHAT YOU CAN'T DO

Many times writers start out just fine, but along the way they begin to struggle, and eventually they come to a full stop. Why does a good start fizzle? Typically this happens because the writer starts to dwell on the trouble spots in the draft and loses momentum. To solve this problem, just skip the trouble spots: If you cannot think of the right word, leave a blank and add it later; if you sense some detail is not working, underline it for later consideration and press on; if the right approach to your introduction escapes you, begin with your second paragraph and go on from there. By focusing on what you *can* do and leaving the problems behind to deal with later, you will make more progress.

RESIST THE TEMPTATION TO REWRITE AS YOU DRAFT

If you constantly rewrite what you have already written, you can become frustrated because you are not moving along quickly enough. Instead, you are stuck in one place—maybe polishing the introduction over and over, or perhaps tinkering endlessly with the detail to support your first point. While some writers do well if they revise as they go, many others get bogged down this way. Instead of forging ahead to discover where their ideas will take them, they keep looking back to where they have been. As a result, getting to the finish line takes too long, and frustration sets in. When you draft, try pushing forward even if what you have already written is in pretty sorry shape. Later you will be able to revise the rough spots.

ALLOW YOUR DRAFT TO BE ROUGH

If you find yourself starting a draft, crumpling up the paper and pitching it to the floor, starting another draft, crumpling up the paper and pitching it to the floor, starting another draft and so forth, you may be expecting too much too soon. Remember, a first draft is supposed to be rough; that's why it is often called a *rough* draft. Instead of wadding up that draft, force yourself to go from start to finish in one sitting to get raw material to shape during the revision process that comes later.

WRITE FAST AND DON'T LOOK BACK

If you write fast, you will have no time to worry about how well you are saying things. You will only be able to get things down the best way you can at the moment. If you don't look back, you won't be tempted to rewrite anything. So write fast, don't look back, and you may be able to push past the block. Later when you revise, you can rework things as needed.

WRITE AN OUTLINE

If you have generated a number of good ideas and you still have trouble writing a draft, the problem may be that you are unsure what idea you should write first, second, third, and so on. An outline can be a great help here. Sometimes a simple scratch outline does the job, so try listing your ideas and then numbering them in the order you will treat them. Other times, a more detailed, formal outline (with roman numerals, letters, and numbers) is called for, particularly if you will treat a number of ideas in considerable depth or if you have a sophisticated plan for development, such as cause-and-effect analysis or comparison and contrast. If you would like more information on outlining, consult Chapter 3.

RETURN TO IDEA GENERATION

It may be that you really do *not* have a clear enough idea of what you want to say, and you need to return to idea generation. Try a favorite idea generation technique to clarify your thinking or to flesh out some existing ideas. Or try a technique you have not used before (see Chapter 2 for suggestions).

THINK POSITIVELY

Positive thinkers outperform negative thinkers. Adopt a positive attitude by thinking of yourself as a writer, as someone who *can and will* get a draft down and revise it successfully.

"I'm Having Trouble with My Introduction."

Beginnings can be difficult. The first day of school, the first day on a new job, a first date—starting out is often hard. Starting out a piece of writing can also be difficult, even if you have generated plenty of ideas before beginning your draft. However, the following strategies can help.

EXPLAIN WHY YOUR TOPIC IS IMPORTANT

Just why should your reader take time to read your essay? If you are having trouble with your introduction, try explaining why your topic is important. For example, say that you are writing to convince your reader that we were wrong to drop the atomic bomb on Hiroshima, Japan, to end World War II. Your introduction could explain that we must understand this issue so we do not repeat such a devastating act:

> Although our bombing of Hiroshima ended World War II, we were wrong to drop the atomic bomb. Until we understand why we were wrong, we are in danger of repeating this devastating action.

PROVIDE BACKGROUND INFORMATION

What must your reader know to appreciate or understand your topic? What information would establish a context for your essay? The answers to these questions can provide background information in the introduction. Assume you plan to argue that public school employees should not be able to strike. Your introduction could supply background information that tells about the strikes in the recent past:

> In 1989, the teachers in a local school system went on strike, successfully closing schools for three full weeks. In 1991, the union representing the custodians and bus drivers went on strike. This time, schools were closed for five days. The system faced another work stoppage in 1992 when the teachers struck for more money; schools were closed two days. Since then, all has been quiet. However, now there is talk of another strike, this time by the non-certified employees. Clearly, it is time to outlaw strikes by public school employees.

TELL A STORY

You can create interest in your topic by telling a story that is related to that topic or that in some way illustrates the point your essay makes. For example, if your essay shows that modern conveniences can be more trouble than they are worth, the following introduction with a story would be effective:

> The morning of my job interview, I woke up an hour earlier than usual and took special pains with my hair and makeup. I ate a light, sensible breakfast which managed to hit bottom despite the menagerie of winged insects fluttering around my stomach. I drove the parkway downtown, nervously biting my lower lip the whole way. I had to park three long blocks from the office building where the interview was to take place, and by the time I got to the building I was completely windblown. Breathless, I gasped my name to the receptionist, who explained that my interview would have to be postponed. The personnel director had never made it in. It seems her electricity was off, and she could not get her car out of the garage because the door was controlled by an electric opener. That's when I knew for sure that modern conveniences can be downright inconvenient.

FIND SOME COMMON GROUND
WITH YOUR READER

Finding common ground with your reader involves identifying a point of view or experience you and your reader share. Presenting this common ground in an introduction can create a bond between reader and writer. In the following introduction, the common ground is a shared school experience:

> Think back to when you were in high school. Remember the kids who caused all the trouble, the ones who disrupted the teacher and made it difficult for the rest of the class to learn? They were the students who did not want to be in school anyway and made things miserable for the students who did want to be there. Now imagine how much more learning would have occurred if the troublemakers had been allowed to quit school and get jobs. If we abolish compulsory attendance, everyone will be better off.

DESCRIBE SOMETHING

Because description adds interest and liveliness to writing, describing something can be an excellent way to begin:

> At 5 feet 3 inches and 170 pounds, Mr. Daria looked like a meatball. His stringy black hair, always in need of a cut, kept sliding into his eyes, and his too-tight shirts would not stay tucked into his too-tight polyester pants. He wore the same sport coat everyday; it was easily identified by the grease splotch on the left lapel. Yes, Mr. Daria was considered a nerd by most of the student body, but to me he was the best history teacher on the planet.

BEGIN WITH THE THESIS AND THE POINTS
YOU WILL DISCUSS

Sometimes the direct approach is the best. You can begin by stating your thesis and the main points you will discuss, like this:

> Carolyn Hotimsky is the best candidate for mayor for two reasons. First, as president of city council, she

demonstrated leadership ability. Second, as chief investment counselor for First City Bank, she learned about sound
fiscal management.

KEEP IT SHORT

If you are having trouble with something, it makes no sense to make it
as long as possible. Thus, if your introduction is proving troublesome,
keep it short. Just write your thesis and one or two other sentences, and
get on with the rest of your writing. If all else fails, just write your thesis and go on to your first point to be developed.

SKIP IT

If you cannot come up with a suitable introduction, skip it for the time
being. Go on to write the rest of your piece and then return to the introduction. With the rest of your writing drafted, you may find that an
approach to your introduction comes to mind. Here's a word of caution, though: If you skip your introduction, jot down a working thesis
on scratch paper and check it periodically to be sure you do not stray
off into unrelated areas.

USE A COMPUTER

If you use a computer, you may like the following techniques.

Windowing.   If you cannot decide which of two or more approaches
to use, windowing can help. To window, execute the command that
lets you divide your screen in half. Then try one approach to your introduction in one-half of the screen and another approach in the other
half. Compare the two approaches and decide which works better.

Turn your conclusion into the introduction.   It may sound strange,
but your last paragraph may work better as an introduction than as a
conclusion. To find out, execute the command that allows you to move
your conclusion to the beginning of your writing. With some fine-tun-
ing, you may be able to turn the conclusion into a strong introduction.
Of course, you will have to write a new conclusion, but that may prove
easier than wrestling with the introduction.

CHAPTER

6

"How Do I Back Up
What I Say?"

You may be a warm, wonderful human being and as honest as they come, but no experienced reader will believe what you say unless you back up your statements with proof and/or explanations. The suggestions in this chapter can help you with this.

TELL A STORY

Search your own experience for brief stories that can drive home your points. Consider this passage, for example:

> Distance running is an excellent sport for adolescents because even if they do not finish near the front of the pack, they can still feel good about themselves. Shaving a few seconds off an earlier time or completing a difficult course can be a genuine source of pride for a young runner.

Now notice how the addition of a brief story helps prove the point:

Distance running is an excellent sport for adolescents because even if they do not finish near the front of the pack, they can still feel good about themselves. Shaving a few seconds off an earlier time or completing a difficult course can be a genuine source of pride for a young runner. I remember a race I ran as a sophomore. I was recovering from a miserable cold and not in peak condition. Just after completing the first mile, I developed a cramp in my side. However, I was determined to finish, no matter how long it took me. Quarter mile by quarter mile, I ran rather haltingly. My chest was tight from lack of training because I had been sick, and my side hurt, but still I kept on. Eventually, I crossed the finish line, well back in the standings. However, I could not have been more proud of myself if I had won. I showed that I had what it took to finish, even though the going was tough.

ADD SOME DESCRIPTION

Look for opportunities to add descriptive detail to your draft. Description allows the writer to create vivid images in the mind of the reader. These images help the reader to see and hear the way the writer sees and hears. They also add considerable interest and vitality to writing. Consider this passage, for example:

The best teacher I ever had was Mrs. Suarez, who taught me algebra in the ninth grade. But even more than teaching me algebra, Mrs. Suarez showed me compassion during a very difficult time in my life. I will always be grateful for her understanding and encouragement when I needed them most.

In the ninth grade, I was a troubled teen, a victim of a difficult home life. Somehow Mrs. Suarez recognized my pain and approached me one day. . . .

Now notice the interest created with the addition of description:

The best teacher I ever had was Mrs. Suarez, who taught me algebra in the ninth grade. But even more than teaching me algebra, Mrs. Suarez showed me compassion during a very difficult time in my life. To look at this woman, a person would never guess what a caring nature she had. With wire-stiff hair teased and lacquered into a bouffant,

Mrs. Suarez looked like a hard woman. Her face, heavily wrinkled, had a scary, witchlike quality that befit the shrill voice she used to reprimand fourteen-year-old sinners who neglected their homework. She always stood ramrod straight with her 120 pounds evenly distributed over her orthopedic shoes. Many a freshman has been frightened by a first look at this no-nonsense woman. However, appearances are, indeed, deceptive, for Mrs. Suarez was not the witch she looked to be. In fact, I will always be grateful for her understanding and encouragement when I needed them most.

PROVIDE EXAMPLES

Readers welcome examples because they make a point so much easier to understand. Thus, when you are looking to back up points, identify ideas that can be made clearer with the addition of a well-chosen example. Assume, for example, that you have written this thesis: "Television commercials do more harm than good." Let's also say that to develop that thesis you make the point that TV commercials cause people to want products they do not need. You could back up that point with examples, like this:

Television commercials often make people want products they do not need. For example, Tony the Tiger urges children to eat highly sugared cereal, while gorgeous, bikini-clad women romp on the beach, luring men to consume beer. Before Christmas, expensive toys based on the latest action hero are advertised relentlessly, until children are convinced they cannot survive without them. Of course, the worst offenders are the advertisers of hair dye, mascara, lipstick, perfume, and teeth-whiteners, who convince women they cannot be attractive without a drawer full of these products.

GIVE REASONS

Reasons help prove that something is true. Let's say that your point is that final examinations should be eliminated. These reasons could help prove your point: Finals create too much anxiety; they do not really show what a student knows; it is not fair to place considerable emphasis on one examination; some students test poorly. Here is how those reasons might appear in a paragraph:

> Final examinations should be eliminated because they are not a sound educational practice. For one thing, these exams create too much anxiety among students. They worry so much about their performance that they lose sleep, stop eating, and show other signs of stress. Certainly, they cannot demonstrate what they know under such circumstances. They also cannot show what they really know because the tests cannot test all of a body of knowledge—just what the teacher wants to test. As a result, some of what a student knows may never be asked for. Furthermore, if the test is poorly constructed (and many of them are), students may further be kept from demonstrating their real learning. Then there is the fact that many students are poor test-takers. They may know the material just fine but be incapable of demonstrating their knowledge because they have never mastered the art of test-taking.

SHOW SIMILARITIES OR DIFFERENCES

If your point is that children with AIDS should not be kept out of schools, then you might compare children with AIDS to those with cancer and note that cancer patients are not kept out of schools. If your point is that children with AIDS *should* be kept out of schools, then set up a contrast: Unlike cancer, AIDS is a communicable disease. The following paragraphs show how to present these similarities and differences.

Comparison

> We should not keep children with AIDS out of school just because they have a catastrophic disease. After all, we do not keep children with cancer out of school, even if their prognosis is as bleak as that for children with AIDS. Just as we try to meet the special needs of cancer victims, we should try to meet the needs of AIDS patients. Only our unreasonable fear stands in the way.

Contrast

> Although we allow children with cancer to stay in school, we cannot do the same for children with AIDS be-

cause unlike cancer, AIDS is a communicable disease. In short, by allowing AIDS patients in our schools, we would put healthy children at risk. In addition, students and teachers would be so afraid of the child with AIDS that fear would take over the classroom and little learning would occur. On the other hand, people are not likely to fear a student with cancer.

EXPLAIN CAUSES OR EFFECTS

If your point is that sex education should be mandatory in all public schools, you can back up your point by citing the positive effects of sex education: Increased knowledge about birth control will lead to fewer teenage pregnancies and hold down the spread of sexually transmitted diseases. If you want to explain why teenagers are sexually active at an early age, you can cite causes: sexy music videos, graphic movies, explicit music lyrics, less emphasis on religion in the home, and so forth. Here are examples:

Cause

One reason teenagers are sexually active at a younger age is that they are bombarded by sexual messages. On MTV, videos are populated with women wearing next to nothing; men and women are touching, groping, and grinding in sexually provocative ways. On the radio, rock lyrics glorify teen sex as healthy rebellion and a sign of independence. Movies, too, send sexual messages. Sex scenes and nudity are frequent in PG-13 movies and are standard fare in R-rated movies that teens get into with no trouble at all. Much of the sex and nudity are unnecessary. For example, Doc Hollywood, rated PG-13, has a lengthy scene of a woman bathing nude in a lake. Nothing would have been lost if the woman had been swimming in the lake instead—with her bathing suit on.

Effect

Sex education's most obvious benefit is increased knowledge. Since it is unlikely that sexually active teens will start to abstain, increased knowledge about birth control will prevent unwanted pregnancy. Furthermore, the same knowledge can help teens protect themselves against sexually transmitted disease. When fewer teens become pregnant, more of them will stay in school and thus will not fall victim to unemployment, drugs, and crime. When more teens protect themselves against sexually transmitted diseases, fewer will die.

EXPLAIN HOW SOMETHING IS MADE OR DONE

Assume you are discussing simple things people can do to combat prejudice. If you make the point that people do not have to put up with racial, ethnic, or sexist humor, you might back up that point by explaining how a person can deal with such humor, like this:

Many people do not know how to respond when they are told a racial, ethnic, or sexist joke, so they smile or laugh politely, even though they feel uncomfortable. A better approach is to say something simple, such as, "I don't find such jokes funny." Then, you can quickly turn the conversation to some neutral topic. If the joke was told to several people, and you do not want to embarrass the speaker, draw him or her aside later and say, "I'm sure you did not mean to, but you made me very uncomfortable when you told your joke." Both of these approaches let the speaker know that hurtful jokes are not universally welcome.

EXPLAIN WHAT WOULD HAPPEN IF YOUR VIEW WERE NOT ADOPTED

Let's say that you are arguing that Candidate A should be elected. To make your point, you can explain what would happen if Candidate A were *not* elected: perhaps higher taxes, an increased trade deficit, and more governmental interference.

If McKenzie is not elected, the future will be bleak for the country. First, McKenzie's opponent has already announced a desire to raise taxes, so we will be forced to give up even more of our hard-earned income. In addition, failure to elect McKenzie will result in an increased trade deficit, since McKenzie's opponent is opposed to tariffs. Thus, our national debt will increase beyond its already outrageous level. Finally, if we do not elect McKenzie, we will face increased government interference, because McKenzie's opponent has announced a desire to return to the government style of the seventies.

"I Don't Know How
to End."

Imagine this: You go to the movies and pay $7.00 to see *The Texas Chainsaw Massacre of Freddy Kruger on Friday the 13th, Part 12.* The beginning is wonderful—you're on the edge of your seat; the middle is very exciting—you're completely caught up in the plot. Then the ending comes—and it's awful. When you walk out of the theater, you probably do not talk about how good the beginning and middle were. Instead, you probably complain about how bad the ending was. Why? Because endings are important. They form the last impression, the one that is most remembered.

Writers must realize that their conclusions form their readers' final impressions. If you write a weak conclusion, no matter how strong the rest of your piece is, your reader will feel let down. Therefore, if you have trouble ending your writing, consult the strategies in this chapter.

EXPLAIN THE SIGNIFICANCE
OF YOUR MAIN POINT

Anything appearing in the conclusion is emphasized because of its placement at the end, where it is most likely to be remembered.

Therefore, the conclusion can be the best place for indicating the significance of your point. For example, let's say your essay told the story of the time you were cut from the junior high school basketball team. Your conclusion can explain the significance of the event, like this:

> Because being cut from the team shattered my self-esteem at such a young age, I have struggled all my life with feelings of inadequacy. I have doubted my ability because the coach, whose judgment I trusted, told me that I didn't have what it takes.

PROVIDE A SUMMARY IF YOUR READER WILL APPRECIATE ONE

Summarizing your main points is a service to your reader if you have written a long piece or one with complex ideas. After reading a long or complicated writing, a reader will appreciate a review of the high points at the end. However, if your piece is short or if the ideas are easily grasped, your reader may find a summary a boring rehash of previously covered material.

EXPLAIN THE CONSEQUENCES OF IGNORING YOUR VIEW

If you are writing to persuade your reader to think or act a certain way, you can close effectively by explaining what would happen if your reader did not follow your recommendation. Assume, for example, that you are writing to convince your reader that a drug education program should be instituted in the local elementary school. After giving your reasons for this view, you could close like this:

> If we do not have a drug education program in the earliest grades, we miss the opportunity to influence our children when they are the most impressionable. If we miss this opportunity to influence them when they are young and responsive to adult pressure, we run the risk of losing our children to powerful peer pressure to experiment with drugs.

CONCLUDE WITH A POINT YOU WANT TO EMPHASIZE

Because the conclusion forms your reader's final impression, anything placed at the end is emphasized. Therefore, you can conclude with your most important point, the one you want underscored in your reader's mind. For example, if you are explaining the differences between child-rearing practices of today and those of fifty years ago, you could end like this:

> Perhaps the most telling difference between child-rearing practices of today and those of fifty years ago is that today's parents are less rigid. Unlike the parents of fifty years ago, they are less concerned with doing everything on schedule and by the book. Babies are not forced to eat and sleep at specific times but may do so when they are hungry and sleepy. Today's parents trust their instincts more than they trust the child-care book used by parents of the past. Thus, they are more likely to do what they think is right and not worry about what the "authorities" say.

RESTATE YOUR THESIS FOR EMPHASIS

Repeating something can be effective if it provides emphasis, but repetition can be boring and annoying if the emphasis is uncalled for. Thus, if you decide to close by restating your thesis, be sure the restatement is effective emphasis rather than boring repetition.

KEEP IT SHORT

If you are having trouble with your conclusion, then keep it short. You do not want to end abruptly, but you also should not take something that is a problem and stretch it out longer than necessary. A perfectly acceptable conclusion can be only one or two sentences.

CHAPTER

8

"I Can't Think of the Right Word."

You're writing along, and just as your confidence begins to surge—wham! Suddenly, you're stuck because you can't think of the right word. You try all the usual techniques—chewing on the end of your pencil to squeeze the word into the tip, rubbing your forehead to massage the word into your brain, and staring at the page to will the word to appear—but nothing helps. Soon it's a matter of pride, and you refuse to budge until you think of the word that's lurking annoyingly just at the tip of your tongue. The next thing you know, fifteen minutes have passed, you have made no progress, and you are frustrated.

When the word you need escapes you, you can avoid becoming frustrated and stalled by trying some of the techniques described in this chapter.

WRITE IN A NATURAL STYLE

You may have trouble finding the right word if you are writing in an unnatural style. Instead of writing with your own normal vocabulary, you may be straining for an overly "sophisticated" style, a style you think will impress the reader. As a result, words escape you because you are seeking ones that were never a natural part of your vocabulary in the first place. Thus, if you find yourself at a loss for words, return to a more natural style, and words should come more easily.

USE ITTS

ITTS stands for *"I'm trying to say."* When you cannot find the right word, stop for a moment and say to yourself, "I'm trying to say ____." Imagine yourself explaining what you mean to a friend and fill in the blank with the word or words you would speak to that friend. Then write the word or words in your draft. You may use several words or even a sentence to fill in the blank when originally you were only seeking a single word. That's fine.

SUBSTITUTE A PHRASE OR A SENTENCE FOR A TROUBLESOME WORD

If you cannot take one path, then take an alternate route to your destination: If you cannot think of the right word, then try using a phrase or a whole sentence to express your idea instead.

ASK AROUND

If you cannot think of the word that is on the tip of your tongue, then ask around. To anyone who will listen, just say, "Hey, what's the word for ____?" Writers are always glad to help each other out of a tight spot.

FREEWRITE FOR THREE MINUTES

You may not be able to think of the right word because you are not certain about what you want to say. To clarify your thinking, try three minutes of freewriting, focusing on the idea you want the word to convey. (Freewriting is explained on page 17.) After the freewriting, try again to come up with the word. You may be able to do so with a better understanding of what you want to express.

SKIP THE PROBLEM AND RETURN TO IT LATER

When you are drafting, never let any one trouble spot stop your progress. If after a minute you cannot think of the right word, then leave a blank space and push on. You can return to consider the problem again when you revise. When you return, the word may surface, and the problem will be solved. If not, you can try the other strategies in this chapter.

USE SIMPLE, SPECIFIC WORDS

Some people have trouble finding the right words because they think good writing has words like *bumptious, egregious, panacea, parsimonious,* and *pusillanimous* in it. The truth is that good writing is clear, simple, and specific. You do not need the high-flown, fifty-dollar words. Instead of *parsimonious,* use *stingy.*

USE THE THESAURUS AND DICTIONARY WISELY

The thesaurus and dictionary are excellent tools for writers seeking the right word. In fact, you may want to invest in a hardback and paperback version of each of these resources. Keep the hardbacks on your writing desk, and carry the paperbacks around with you. One word of caution is in order, however. Be sure you understand the connotation (secondary meaning) of any word you draw from these sources. For example, *skinny* and *lean* may mean the same thing on one level, but because of their connotations, a person would rather be called *lean* than *skinny.* If you do not understand the connotations of a word, you run a risk of misusing it.

USE A COMPUTER

Some word processing programs come with a built-in thesaurus. If yours does not, you can purchase an add-on thesaurus program. Such a program can be handy, but you must be sure you understand the meaning of any word you take from this source.

Revising

Because writers usually produce drafts that require a substantial amount of reworking, you will need to study your draft carefully and objectively to discover ways to improve the content, organization, and expression of ideas. This kind of reworking is revising, and it is hard work; however, the procedures described in this section can help you.

"I Don't Like My Draft."

You've just placed the final period at the end of the last sentence of your first draft, and you're feeling proud of yourself. So you lean back, put your feet up on the desk, and start to reread the masterpiece. However, as you read, you start to feel less and less proud—your masterpiece isn't nearly as good as you thought it was. Does this mean you have to start over? Probably not. Instead, try some of the suggestions in this chapter.

BE REALISTIC

Remember that another name for a first draft is a *rough* draft because your first attempt is supposed to have problems—even lots of them. You should not build in frustration by expecting too much too soon. Instead, realize that your first pass is bound to be rough, roll up your sleeves, and get in there and revise until you are happy with the results.

WALK AWAY

Before deciding about the quality of your draft, leave it for a while to clear your head and regain your objectivity. The longer you stay away, the better; but walk away for at least several hours—for a day if you have the time. When you return to your draft and reread it, you may discover potential that you overlooked previously.

SHARE THE DRAFT

Sometimes writers are too hard on themselves in the early drafting stage. Instead of recognizing the potential in their drafts, they see only the rough spots. As a result, they become frustrated and start over when it is not really necessary. Before deciding about the quality of your draft, share it with several people whose judgment you trust. Ask these readers to note all the strengths in the draft and all the areas that can be made strong with some polishing. When you review your readers' comments, you may see how much potential your draft has.

LISTEN TO YOUR DRAFT

Your draft may seem worse than it is if it is messy or written in sloppy handwriting or written in pencil or written on paper ripped out of a spiral notebook. In short, the overall appearance of the draft may affect your evaluation of it. To judge the worth of your draft more reliably, ask someone to read it to you. As you listen, you may discover sections that are far stronger than you realized.

IDENTIFY TWO CHANGES THAT WILL IMPROVE THE DRAFT

If you study your draft and identify two changes that will make it better, you may recognize how much potential your draft has. If you think it will help you judge your draft better, make those changes and *then* decide how you feel about the draft.

TRY TO SALVAGE SOMETHING

If you are sure that your draft is awful and you must begin again, at least try to salvage something. Perhaps you can use the same approach to your introduction, or some of your examples, or one main idea. While it is tempting to rip the draft to shreds and begin anew, you may not have to begin at square 1. Some of your work may be useable in your new draft.

WRITE A SECOND DRAFT WITHOUT LOOKING AT THE FIRST

Writing a second draft without looking at the first is often successful because you manage to retain the best parts of the first draft, eliminate the weakest parts, and add some new, effective material. The key is to avoid checking the first draft while writing the second.

DO NOT DESPAIR IF YOU MUST START OVER

Writers start over all the time because often we must discover what we do *not* want to do before we discover what we *do* want to do; sometimes we must learn what we can*not* do before we are clear about what we *can* do. If you must begin again, do not be discouraged. Your earlier draft or drafts were not a waste of your time—they were groundwork, preliminary efforts that paved the way for your most recent effort.

DO THE BEST YOU CAN WITH WHAT YOU HAVE

Yes, writers start over all the time, but writers do not usually have an unlimited amount of time to work within. At some point you must force yourself to push forward, even if you are not completely comfortable with the status of your first draft. Not every piece can be a shining moment, so when time is running out, do the best you can with what you have and be satisfied that you have met your deadline.

CHAPTER

10

"I Don't Know What to Change."

Good news! You finished your first draft, and you are ready to dig in and make all those changes that will improve your writing and make it fit for a reader. So you read your draft—but wait a minute—everything seems fine. *You* understand what you mean; everything seems clear and well developed to *you*. In fact, you can't figure out what changes to make. Well, the truth is that as the writer you may have no trouble at all figuring out what you meant when you wrote all those words, but that does not guarantee that the reader will have an easy time of it. In order to revise successfully, you must view your draft as the reader will and make changes to meet your reader's needs. The suggestions in this chapter can help.

WALK AWAY

Before revising, the smartest thing you can do is leave your work for a day, or even longer if you can manage it. Getting away from your writing gives you a chance to clear your head and regain your objectivity so that when you return to revise you stand a better chance of seeing your work the way your reader will.

DESCRIBE YOUR DRAFT PARAGRAPH BY PARAGRAPH

Describing your draft paragraph by paragraph can help you analyze its strengths and weaknesses. To do this, summarize the contents of paragraph 1; then explain how that paragraph meets your audience's needs. Next, summarize the contents of paragraph 2; then explain how that paragraph meets your audience's needs. Continue in this fashion until you have described each paragraph. Reading over your description can help you identify points that stray from your thesis, ideas that need more development, paragraphs that fail to meet a reader's needs, and other problems to work on during revision.

TYPE YOUR DRAFT

If you wrote your draft in pen or pencil, type it into a neat copy and then read it over. Problems that you overlook in your own handwriting may be more apparent in typed form because the copy resembles printed material rather than your own handiwork. As a result, it can be easier to be objective about the writing. Also, some mistakes may leap out at you. For example, a paragraph that ran the better part of a page in your handwritten copy may be only three lines in typed form—a visual signal that more detail may be needed.

LISTEN TO YOUR DRAFT

Many times we can hear problems that we overlook visually. For this reason, writers should read their drafts out loud at least once. When you read aloud, be sure to go slowly and be careful to read exactly what is on the page. If you read quickly, you are likely to read what you *meant* to write rather than what you actually *did* write.

Some writers do well if they read their drafts into a tape recorder. Then they play back the tape to listen for problems.

Still other writers prefer to have other people read their drafts to them. Sometimes, another person's tone of voice helps the writer pick up on problems.

UNDERLINE MAIN POINTS

One way to determine if you have supported your points is to go through your draft and underline every main idea. Then go back and check to see what appears after each underlined point. If one underlined point is immediately followed by another underlined point, you have not supported a main idea. Similarly, if an underlined idea is followed by only one or two sentences, you should consider whether you have enough support. For strategies for supporting points, see Chapter 6.

OUTLINE YOUR DRAFT AFTER WRITING IT

A good way to determine if your ideas follow logically one to the next is to outline your draft *after* writing it. If you have points that do not fit into the outline at the appropriate spots, you have discovered an organization problem.

REVISE IN STAGES

When you revise, you have a great deal to consider—so much, in fact, that you may overlook some things. One way to avoid overlooking important considerations is to revise in stages, following one of these patterns.

Easy to hard.   First make all the easy changes, take a break, and then go on to make the more difficult changes. Take a break whenever you become tired or when you get stuck. Making the easy changes first may help you build enough momentum to carry you through the harder changes.

Hard to easy.   First make some of your more difficult changes, take a break, make some more of your difficult changes, take another break, and continue with the harder changes, taking breaks as needed. When you have finished the more difficult changes, take a break and tackle the easier changes. Some writers like the psychological lift that comes from getting the hard changes out of the way and knowing the rest of revision is downhill.

Paragraph by paragraph.   Revise your first paragraph until it is as perfect as you can make it, and then go on to the next paragraph. Proceed paragraph by paragraph, taking a break after every paragraph or two.

Content–organization–effective expression. First make all your content changes: adequate detail, relevant detail, specific detail, clarity, and suitable introduction and conclusion. Then take a break and check the organization: logical order of ideas, effective thesis, and clear topic sentences. Take another break and revise for sentence effectiveness: effective word choice, smooth flow, helpful transitions.

SHARE YOUR INTRODUCTION AND CONCLUSION

To help you judge the effectiveness of your introduction and conclusion, type up these parts of your writing separately, and give them to two or three people to read. Ask them whether they would be interested in reading something that opened and closed with these paragraphs.

SHARE YOUR DRAFT WITH A RELIABLE READER

If you have trouble deciding what changes to make, ask someone to react to your draft and suggest revisions. To get the most constructive criticism possible, be sure your reader is reliable. That is, be sure your reader is someone who knows about the qualities of effective writing. Also, be sure your reader will not hesitate to offer criticism. If your roommate is afraid of hurting your feelings, do not ask him or her to read your draft. Similarly, if your cousin has failed a writing course twice, do not ask your cousin to react to your draft.

If your school has a writing center, stop in to get a reliable reaction to your draft. Typically, writing center staff members are trained to provide sensitive responses to student writing.

For additional information on getting reader response and for questions a reader can answer, see Appendix 2.

CONSTRUCT A READER PROFILE

A good way to identify changes that should be made in your draft is to consider your detail in light of your reader's point of view. Different readers will place different demands on a writer. For example, assume you are writing to convince your reader to vote for a school levy that will increase property taxes. If your audience is someone with children in the school system, explaining that the additional revenue will go toward enhancing the art and music curriculum may be sufficiently persuasive. However, if your reader is a childless retired person on a fixed income, this argument may not be very convincing. Instead, you may need to explain that better schools will cause the reader's home to increase in value so the resale price is higher.

To evaluate your detail from your reader's point of view, construct a reader profile by answering the following ten questions:

1. How much education does my reader have?

2. What is my reader's age, sex, race, nationality, and religion?

3. What is my reader's occupation and socioeconomic level?

4. What part of the country does my reader live in? Does my reader live in an urban or rural area?

5. What is my reader's political affiliation?

6. How familiar is my reader with my topic?

7. What does my reader need to know to appreciate my point of view?

8. How resistant will my reader be to my point of view?

9. How hard will I have to work to create interest in my topic?

10. Does my reader have any special hobbies or interests or concerns that will affect how my essay is viewed? Is my reader chiefly concerned with money? career? the environment? society? religion? family?

After answering these questions, review your draft with an eye toward providing detail suited to your reader's unique makeup.

PRETEND TO BE SOMEONE ELSE

To be more objective about your work so you can decide what to change, pretend you are someone else. Read your draft as the judge of a contest who will award you $10,000 for a prize-winning essay. Or become the editor of a magazine who is deciding what changes to make in the draft before publishing the piece. Or read as your worst enemy, someone who loves to find fault with your work. Assuming a new personality as you read your draft may help you depersonalize your work enough to allow you to find what should be revised.

USE A REVISING CHECKLIST

To be sure they have covered everything, some writers like to use a checklist when they rework their drafts. If you are such a writer, the following checklist may help. The advantages of the checklist are that it helps you proceed in an orderly way, and it keeps you from over-looking some of the revision concerns. In addition, you can combine this checklist with reader response by asking a reliable reader to apply the checklist to your draft.

The page numbers in parentheses refer you to helpful pages in this book.

Content

1. Does your writing have a clear thesis, either stated or implied, that accurately presents your focus? (page 7)

2. Does every point in your writing clearly relate to that thesis? (page 8)

3. Are all your generalizations, including your thesis, adequately supported? (page 78)

4. Are all your points well suited to your audience, purpose, and role? (pages 4, 5, and 6)

5. Have you avoided stating the obvious? (page 88)

6. Does your introduction create interest in your topic? (page 49)

7. Does your conclusion provide a satisfying ending? (page 59)

Organization

1. Do your ideas follow logically one to the next?

2. Do your paragraphs follow logically one to the next?

3. Do the details in each paragraph relate to the topic sentence? (page 8)

4. Have you used transitions to show how ideas relate to each other? (page 36)

5. Have you outlined? (page 32)

Expression

1. When you read your work aloud, does everything sound all right? (page 71)

2. Have you avoided wordiness? (page 83)

3. Have you eliminated clichés (overworked expressions)? (page 88)

4. Have you used specific words? (page 85)

5. Did you use a variety of sentence openers? (page 90)

6. Did you use ITTS as needed? (page 63)

7. Have you used the active voice? (page 87)

8. Have you used action verbs rather than forms of *be?* (page 87)

TRUST YOUR INSTINCTS

A good way to decide what needs to be changed is to read your draft over and listen to your instincts. When your instincts tell you that something is wrong, you can be reasonably sure that you have come across a problem. Even if you cannot give the problem a name, and even if you are not yet sure what change needs to be made, when you get that feeling that all is not well, assume that you have identified something that needs to be reworked. Most of the time, a writer's instincts are correct.

DO NOT EDIT PREMATURELY

Sometimes writers have trouble deciding what to change because they get bogged down checking commas, spelling, fragments, and the like. However, concerns such as these are matters of correctness, and matters of correctness are best dealt with later, during editing. During revision, you stand a better chance of recognizing what needs to be changed if you focus on content, organization, and effective expression. Do not be distracted by editing concerns too early in the writing process.

USE A COMPUTER

If you wrote your draft on a computer, the following tips may help you decide what changes to make.

Study a print copy of your draft.   You may be better off printing out your draft and studying the print copy. Viewing the text on the screen can be less helpful because you see such small portions at a time that you may have trouble getting a good overview of your writing.

Put a checklist in a window.   If your computer allows you to split the screen, place a revising checklist in a window to refer to as you reread your work. This way, you will be constantly reminded of what to consider while revising. Either make up your own checklist, or copy the one on page 75.

Highlight areas with boldface type.   If you are unsure about parts of your draft—if you don't know whether or not they should be changed—use the boldface function of your word processing program to highlight the areas in question. Then print out your draft and give it to two or more reliable readers (see page 73) and ask them to react to the parts in boldface type.

CHAPTER

"My Draft Is Too Short."

Sometimes you think you have enough ideas to get under way, so you start drafting. Later, you come to the end and place a period after your last sentence. Then you look back over your work, and you come to a disheartening recognition: Your draft is much too short, and you have already said everything you can think of. What do you do? No, you do not throw yourself in front of a high-speed train. Instead, you try one of the strategies in this chapter.

UNDERLINE MAJOR POINTS

Your draft may be too short because you wrote down your major points but neglected to develop them. To determine if this is the case, go through your draft and underline every major point. Then check to see how much you have written after each underlined point. If one underlined point is immediately followed by another underlined point, you have neglected to develop an idea. Adding supporting detail after one or more of your major points can solve your length problem. (See Chapter 6 for ways to add supporting detail.)

When you add detail, be careful not to state the obvious or provide unrelated information, or you will be guilty of *padding*—writing useless material just to bulk up the piece. Padding is a problem because it irritates readers by requiring them to read unnecessary material. Let's assume that you are writing to explain how schools foster competition, rather than cooperation, in students. If you were to say that schools have students compete for grades, compete for positions on sports teams, compete for student government, compete for scholarships, and compete for cheerleading, you would be providing helpful examples that illustrate your point. However, if you were to give a dictionary definition of *competition* as "the act of struggling to win some prize, honor, or advantage," you would be padding your essay with information your reader already knows.

SHOW AFTER YOU TELL

If your draft is too short, you may be *telling* your reader things are true without *showing* that they are true. A good rule to remember is "show; don't just tell." Consider the following:

> I have always hated winter. For one thing, the cold bothers me. For another, daily living becomes too difficult.

The previous sentences are an example of telling without showing. Here is a revision with detail added to *show:*

> I have always hated winter. For one thing, the cold bothers me. Even in the house with the furnace running, I can never seem to get warm. I wear a turtleneck under a heavy wool sweater and drink one cup of hot tea after another in a futile effort to ease the chill that goes to my bones. A simple trip to the mailbox at the street leaves me chattering for an hour. My hands go numb, and my nose and ears sting from the cold. The doctor explained that I cannot tolerate the cold because I have a circulation problem which causes my capillaries to spasm, interrupting the blood flow to my extremities. I also hate winter because daily living becomes too difficult. Snow and ice are tracked into the house, necessitating frequent cleanups. Snow must be shoveled to get the car out of the driveway. Icy walks make walking treacherous, and driving to the grocery store becomes a dangerous endeavor thanks to slick, snow-covered roads.

See the difference showing—instead of just telling—can make?

☞ *Note: For ways to show rather than just tell, consult Chapter 6.*

RETURN TO IDEA GENERATION

Your draft may be too short because you began writing before you generated enough ideas to write about. This is really not a problem; simply interrupt your drafting for a while and go back to generating ideas. If you have a favorite idea generation technique, try it now. If it lets you down, try one or more of the other techniques described in Chapter 2. Writers frequently step back to idea generation before going forward, so interrupting your drafting is not something you should either resist or worry about.

CHECK YOUR THESIS

If you have tried the previous techniques for fleshing out your draft, and you still do not have enough material, study your thesis to see if it too severely limits the territory you can cover. If so, broaden the thesis a bit so that you can cover more ground and thereby increase the length of your draft.

Let's say, for example, that your draft has this thesis:

```
High school athletics teaches adolescents to be self-
reliant.
```

If you have exhausted everything you can say about how high school athletics teaches self-reliance, if you have tried all the techniques in this chapter, and if you still only have a page and a half of material, consider expanding your thesis to allow discussion of other points:

```
High school athletics teaches adolescents to be self-
reliant. Interestingly, however, athletics also teaches
young people how to be team players.
```

Now you can expand the draft by discussing two advantages of high school athletics rather than one.

A word of caution is in order here: Do not get carried away when you expand your thesis, or you will be forced into covering too much territory. Consider how difficult it would be to provide an adequately detailed discussion of this expanded thesis:

> High school athletics teaches adolescents everything they need to know to succeed as adults: how to be self-reliant, how to be a team player, how to function under pressure, how to accept criticism, and how to give 100 percent.

An essay with this thesis is destined to fail in one of two ways. Either it will be so long that the reader will feel overwhelmed, or it will provide only superficial treatment of the main points.

USE A COMPUTER

Go through your draft, and before each of your main points press the insert key and then hit the space bar ten times. This should visually separate each main point and its support. Once each main point and support are separated from the rest of the essay, you can study each point and support individually to determine if you can add an example, a story, or some description. After adding detail to develop the main points, rejoin your sentences to form a longer draft.

CHAPTER

12

"My Draft Is Too Long."

Perhaps you find yourself writing page after page after page after page—all the while feeling great because you have so much to say. Unfortunately, longer is not necessarily better. In fact, you should keep in mind that your reader's time is valuable and thus keep your writing to a length that will not unduly tax your audience. If, nevertheless, you find that your draft is too long, try one or more of the strategies listed here.

CHECK YOUR THESIS

Look for ways to narrow the scope of your thesis. If your thesis takes in too much territory, you will be forced to cover too many points, and the result will be a very long piece of writing. Here is a thesis that calls for a very long piece:

> The amount of violence on television, in the movies, and in popular fiction is alarming.

To discuss television, movie, and book violence in adequate detail would require many, many pages. A more manageable piece of writing would result from a thesis like this:

```
The amount of violence in prime-time network television is
alarming.
```

ELIMINATE UNNECESSARY POINTS

Writers sometimes forget to consider what their readers already know, and as a result, their writing tends to overexplain. For example, assume you are writing a report on the mutual funds that provide the best retirement income. If you are writing for your boss, who is an investment banker, it would be silly to define the term *mutual funds.* However, if you are writing a newspaper article for readers who may not know what mutual funds are, a definition would be helpful. Similarly, if you are comparing two kinds of bicycles, you should not mention that both have two tires, as this would be stating the obvious.

If your draft is too long, check to be sure you are not making unnecessary points.

OUTLINE YOUR DRAFT

Even if you outlined before drafting, outline your draft after you write it. Then check the outline to be sure you are not repeating points or including irrelevant detail.

ELIMINATE WORDINESS

Often you can cut your draft down to size by eliminating wordiness in the following ways:

1. Eliminate repetition.

```
Wordy:   My biggest problem and concern was how to pay next
         month's rent. (Problem and concern are repetitious.)
Better:  My biggest problem was how to pay next month's rent.
Better:  My biggest concern was how to pay next month's rent.
```

2. Eliminate deadwood (words that add no meaning).

Wordy: I cannot concentrate unless I am alone by myself.
(*Alone* includes the idea *by myself.*)

Better: I cannot concentrate unless I am alone.

Better: I cannot concentrate unless I am by myself.

DO NOT OVERWRITE YOUR INTRODUCTION OR CONCLUSION

If your draft is too long, check your introduction and conclusion to be sure one or both are not overly long. Remember, these two parts of an essay are not meant to do anything more than pave the way for your main discussion and tie things off at the end.

CHAPTER

13

"My Writing Seems Boring."

"I couldn't put it down!" "A real page-turner!" "A must read!" No, these are not the exclamations people must make about your writing, but you do have a responsibility to hold your reader's interest. If your draft seems boring, try the strategies described in this chapter.

REPLACE GENERAL WORDS WITH SPECIFIC ONES

To make your writing more interesting, replace general words with more specific ones. Here are two sentences. The first has general words, which are underlined; the second has specific words, which are also underlined. Which sentence is more interesting?

General words: The <u>car went</u> down the <u>street</u>.
Specific words: The <u>red Corvette streaked</u> down <u>Dover Avenue</u>.

You probably found the second sentence more interesting because of its more specific word choice. To make your sentences more interest-

ing, go through your draft and circle every general word. Then replace
some of those words with more specific words or phrases. The following chart will give you a clearer idea of the difference between general
and specific words.

General	Specific	General	Specific
car	1989 Buick	dog	mangy collie
sweater	yellow cardigan	hat	Phillies cap
shoes	Nike hightops	movie	*Forrest Gump*
feel good	feel optimistic	book	*Misery*
walk	saunter	drink	slurp
cry	sob loudly	said	snapped suddenly
house	two-story colonial	rain	pounding rain
a lot	twelve	later	in two days

ADD DESCRIPTION

Description adds vitality and interest, so if your draft seems boring,
look for opportunities to describe something: a scene, a person's cloth-
ing, a facial expression, a tone of voice, the brightness of the sun, the
feel of a handshake. The description need not be elaborate, nor should
it distract the reader from your main point. For example, if you are
telling the story of a first encounter, some description can add liveliness, like this:

> The door was open and I saw Dr. Harkness hunched over
> his desk, his nose on the paper he was studying, his eyes
> squinted into slits. I knocked on the door frame to get
> his attention, but the barely perceptible sound was too
> much for him. He jerked upright, startled by the intru-
> sion. When he saw me, he brushed wisps of white hair from
> his eyes, smoothed his red and blue flannel shirt, and
> smiled sheepishly. "How can I help you, young man?" he
> asked, as he lifted his bulky frame from the chair.

ADD SPECIFIC EXAMPLES

Examples add interest because they take the general and make it specific. If your draft seems boring, look for opportunities to follow a gen-

eral point with a specific example. For instance, if you say that Lee is a scatterbrain, go on to show this by giving the example of the time Lee locked the keys in the car three times in one day.

TELL A STORY

A brief story can add interest and vitality, and it can help establish a point by serving as an example. For instance, assume you are explaining that being a student *and* a parent can get very complicated. Also assume that one point you make is that sometimes the two roles conflict with each other. To establish this point, you could tell the story of the time your six-year-old woke up sick three hours before your history exam and you had to get her to the doctor, arrange for a baby-sitter, and pick up a prescription—and still make it to class on time.

USE THE ACTIVE VOICE

To give your writing more energy, rewrite sentences so that their subjects perform the actions indicated by the verbs. Then your sentences will be in the *active voice.* Here is an example:

`The labor leader negotiated a new contract for the auto-workers.` (The action suggested by the verb *negotiated* is performed by the subject, *labor leader.*)

When the subject does not perform the verb's action, the sentence has less energy:

`The new contract for the autoworkers was negotiated by the labor leader.` (The subject *the new contract* does not perform the action of the verb *negotiated.*)

SUBSTITUTE ACTION VERBS FOR FORMS OF <u>TO BE</u>

Forms of *to be (am, is, are, was, were)* have less energy and interest than action verbs do, so when possible use action verbs instead of these forms, like this:

Less energy: Mayor Daley <u>was</u> always a believer in party politics.

More energy: Mayor Daley always <u>believed</u> in party politics.

REWRITE CLICHÉS

Clichés are tired, overworked expressions. At one time they were fresh and interesting, but because of overuse, they have become boring. Here is a representative sampling of clichés:

cold as ice	free as a bird	sadder but wiser
high as a kite	last but not least	old as the hills
fresh as a daisy	stiff as a board	hard as nails
under the weather	bull in a china shop	raining cats and dogs
in the same boat	the last straw	smart as a whip

   If your draft seems boring, look for clichés. Each time you find one, underline it. Then, to add interest, replace the clichés with original phrasings. Here is an example:

Cliché: When the police officer pulled me over for speeding, I was shaking like a leaf.

Revision: When the police officer pulled me over for speeding, I was trembling with anxiety.

ELIMINATE STATEMENTS OF THE OBVIOUS

Stating the obvious can make an otherwise strong piece of writing seem boring. Let's say that you are arguing that young people should not be permitted to watch more than an hour of television a day. A sentence like the following will bore a reader because some of what it says is so obvious it does not need to be said at all.

Television, an electronic device for bringing sound and pictures into the home, can be a positive or negative influence on our children, depending on how it is used.

To make your writing more interesting, eliminate statements of the obvious:

```
Television can be a positive or negative influence on our
children, depending on how it is used.
```

CHECK YOUR THESIS

If your thesis takes in too much territory, you can be forced into a superficial, general discussion—and such discussions are boring. For example, consider this thesis:

```
Professional sports should be reformed.
```

An essay that adequately covers all professional sports and all areas that could benefit from reform is likely to involve a superficial discussion because anything in-depth will lead to a very long piece. If your writing is boring because your discussion is too general, look at what you are trying to cover. If your thesis is ambitious, pare it down, like this:

```
During the playing season, athletes should have to submit
to random drug testing.
```

Now you can provide a much more interesting discussion because you can give specifics and still have a piece that is a manageable length.

USE A COMPUTER

Use your word processing program's search-and-replace function to find general words you are in the habit of using. For example, you can ask the computer to spot where you have used these general words: *very, quite, a lot, rather, really, great, good, bad,* and *some.* Once the computer has located these words, you can decide whether to retain one or more of them or rewrite to be more specific.

"My Writing Sounds Choppy."

Read this paragraph out loud. It sounds choppy. The style seems immature. The writing does not sound like it was written by a forty-two-year-old woman with a couple of college degrees. It sounds like it was written by someone's kid brother. This is my way of showing that choppiness is bad. Is it working?

Actually, you do not always have to read your work aloud to detect choppiness. When you read silently, the words "sound" in your brain, allowing you to "hear" this problem. Once you detect choppiness, you can eliminate it with the techniques described in this chapter.

USE DIFFERENT SENTENCE OPENERS

Your writing will sound choppy or singsong if too many sentences in a row all begin in the same way. For example, the first paragraph of this chapter sounds choppy because most of the sentences begin with the subject. The solution to the problem is to mix up sentence openings by trying some of the suggestions that follow.

1. Open with a descriptive word (a modifier).

Strangely, little Billy did not enjoy his birthday.

Confused, the stranger asked directions to the nearest hotel.

Melting, the ice formed slushy puddles on the pavement.

2. Open with a descriptive phrase (a modifier).

Despite my better judgment, I bought a ticket for the roller coaster ride.

Hiding in the living room, twelve of us waited for the right moment to leap out and yell, "Surprise!"

Pleased by her grade on the physics exam, Loretta treated herself to a special dinner.

Under the couch, the wet dog hid from her owner.

3. Open with a subordinate clause (a dependent word group with a subject and verb).

When Congress announced its budget reform package, members of both political parties offered their support.

If the basketball team can recruit a power forward, we will have all the ingredients for a winning season.

Before you contribute to a charity, check the identification of the person requesting the money.

4. Open with to and the verb (an infinitive).

To protect our resources, we must make recycling a way of life.

To convince my parents to buy me a car, I had to agree to pay the car insurance.

To gain five pounds by the start of wrestling season, Luis doubled his intake of carbohydrates.

5. Open with the subject.

Losses led gains in today's stock market activity.

Corvina's goal is to become the youngest manager in the company's history.

The curtains were dulled by years of accumulated dirt.

VARY THE PLACEMENT OF TRANSITIONS

Transitions are words and phrases that link ideas and show how they relate to each other. (Transitions are discussed on page 36.) One way to eliminate choppiness is to vary the placement of transitions in your sentences.

Transition
at the beginning: In addition, providing child care in the workplace is a good idea because half of all mothers now work.

Transition
in the middle: Jan's opinion, on the other hand, is that child-care programs will cost too much money.

Transition
at the end: Many employers now offer day care as a benefit, however.

COMBINE SHORT SENTENCES

When you hear choppiness, look to see if you have two or more short sentences in a row. If so, combine at least two of those short sentences into a longer one, using one of these words:

and	nor	yet
but	for	because
or	so	

Short sentences
(choppy):   The house was well constructed. It was decorated badly.

Combined sentence
(smoother):   The house was well constructed, but it was decorated badly.

Short sentences
(choppy):   The police and fire fighters both needed money. They combined their resources in a fund-raiser.

Combined sentence
    (smoother):   `The police and fire fighters both needed money, so they combined their resources in a fund-raiser.`

FOLLOW LONG SENTENCES WITH SHORT ONES
AND SHORT SENTENCES WITH LONG ONES

The following examples alternate long and short sentences. As you read them, notice how well they flow as a result of the variation in length.

Short followed
    by long: `The coach jumped to his feet. Although he had been coaching for over twenty-five years, he had never before seen such a perfectly exe-cuted play.`

Long followed
    by short: `This city needs a mayor who knows how to deal effectively with city council and how to trim waste from the municipal budget. This city needs Dale Davidson.`

USE YOUR EAR

A good way to discover if parts of your writing are choppy is to read aloud with a pen in your hand. Where you hear that your writing is not flowing well, place a check mark. (Pay particular attention to the flow from one paragraph to the next.) Then go back and try the techniques described in this chapter to ease the flow where you have placed the check marks.

USE A COMPUTER

Use the insert function of your word processing program to add six spaces before and after each sentence in your draft. With your sentences separated from each other, you can check length and openings and revise as necessary. When done, just delete the extra spaces to bring your sentences back together again.

P A R T

Editing

Errors in grammar, spelling, punctuation, and capitalization present a special problem because if you make too many mistakes, your reader will lose confidence in your ability. For this reason, you have a responsibility to find and correct your errors. This process is editing. For most writers, it makes sense to edit last, after all the other changes have been made. This way you are not checking something that you may ultimately strike from the paper anyway. When you do edit, the procedures described in the next chapters can help.

CHAPTER

"I Have Trouble Finding My Mistakes."

You finished your piece, so off it goes to your reader. But when your audience reads your writing, you feel deflated because your eagle-eyed reader found lots of mistakes you never noticed. On closer look, you become frustrated because you now see the same mistakes yourself. Why does that misspelled word leap out at you now when it went unnoticed before? Why is that incorrect verb form so obvious now when it was invisible earlier?

The truth is, writers often overlook their mistakes if they do not take special pains to find them, using the techniques in this chapter.

EDIT LAST

The most efficient time to edit (find and correct mistakes) is near the end of your writing process, after you have made your revisions in content, organization, and wording. If you edit before revising, you may look up the spelling of a word that you later eliminate during revision, check a comma in a sentence that never makes the final draft, and so forth.

Also, you may have trouble finding your mistakes if you edit too soon, when your mind is really concerned with larger matters. For example, locating and eliminating sentence fragments is difficult to do if at the same time you are concerned about supporting a point. Thus, if you have trouble finding your mistakes, be sure you save editing for last, when you can focus all your concentration on it.

LEAVE YOUR WORK FOR A WHILE

By the time you are ready to look for errors, you will have spent a significant amount of time on your writing. In fact, you may not have a fresh enough perspective to notice mistakes. To compensate for this fact, you should leave your writing for a day to clear your head. When you return to your work, you should have a sharper eye for spotting errors.

POINT TO EACH WORD AND PUNCTUATION MARK

To find your mistakes, you must go over your writing *very* slowly. If you build up even a little speed, you will probably overlook errors because you will see what you *intended* to write rather than what you actually *did* write. This is because you know so well what you want to say that you tend to see it on the page whether it is there or not. One way to ensure that you move slowly is to point to each word and punctuation mark and study each one a second or two. Be sure to read what you are pointing to; it is tempting to move your finger or pen ahead of what you are reading, which causes you to build up too much speed and miss mistakes.

USE A RULER

Place a ruler under the first line of your writing and examine that line one word at a time for mistakes. Then drop the ruler down a line and examine that line for mistakes. If you move through your entire piece of writing this way, you may have better luck finding errors for two reasons. First, you are less likely to build up too much speed and miss mistakes. Second, the ruler prevents the words below the line from entering your visual field and distracting you.

PREPARE A FRESH, TYPED COPY OF YOUR DRAFT

Because handwriting can be hard on the eyes, errors can be spotted more easily in typed copy. Also, you can be more objective about typed copy because it seems more like printed material—more like someone else's writing.

LISTEN TO YOUR DRAFT

Sometimes you can hear mistakes that you overlook visually. For this reason, you should listen to your writing. Have someone read your draft to you, or read it aloud to yourself, or speak it into a tape recorder and play back the tape. If you read your draft to yourself or into a tape recorder, be sure to read *exactly* what is on the page. Remember, writers tend to read what they *meant* to say rather than what they *did* say. Also, remember that some mistakes, such as certain misspellings, cannot be heard, so listening should be combined with one or more of the visual editing strategies.

LEARN YOUR PATTERN OF ERROR

We all make mistakes, but we do not all make the *same* mistakes. One person may misspell words often, another may write run-on sentences, another may have trouble choosing the correct verb, and so on. Be aware of the kinds of mistakes you make so you can make a special effort to locate those errors. In fact, edit one extra time for each of the mistakes you have a tendency to make.

Once you know the kinds of mistakes you make, you may be able to determine under what circumstances you make those mistakes. For example, once you discover that you have trouble choosing verbs, a little study of your writing may tell you that you have this trouble whenever you begin a sentence with *there is* or *there are.* This is valuable information because it tells you to check the verbs in any sentences that begin with these words.

To tune in to your pattern of error, keep a log of your mistakes so you can check which ones occur with the greatest frequency. If you keep a journal (see page 25), you can record on a back page the kinds of mistakes you make by checking the instructor comments on your evaluated essays.

USE AN EDITING CHECKLIST

One way to be sure you are editing thoroughly is to use a checklist. The one below may meet your needs. If you prefer, devise your own checklist of errors you are in the habit of making.

☞ *Note: The page numbers in parentheses refer you to helpful pages in the book.*

1. Have you read your work aloud to listen for problems? (page 99)

2. Did you check every possible misspelling in a dictionary or with a spell checker? (page 138)

3. Did you edit for run-on sentences and comma splices? (page 109)

4. Did you edit for sentence fragments? (page 103)

5. Did you check your use of verbs? (page 121)

6. Did you check your use of pronouns? (page 113)

7. Did you check your use of modifiers? (page 126)

8. Have you checked any punctuation you are unsure of? (pages 131 and 134)

9. Have you checked your use of capital letters?

TRUST YOUR INSTINCTS

Maybe you have had this experience: You have a nagging feeling that something is wrong. However, you cannot give the problem a name, and you are not sure how to solve it, so you just skip over it and hope your reader does not notice. Then you submit your writing, and sure enough—your reader was troubled by the same thing you were troubled by. If you have had this experience, you learned that your instincts are reliable. When that nagging feeling tells you a problem exists, trust the feeling and assume that something is wrong. Because much of what you know about language has been internalized, an inner alarm may sound when you have made a mistake. Always heed that alarm, even if you are not sure what the problem is or how to solve it. Get help if necessary for diagnosing and eliminating the error.

EDIT MORE THAN ONCE

Because it is so easy to overlook errors, you should edit more than once. Many writers like to edit once for anything they can find and a separate time for each of the kinds of errors they have a tendency to make.

LEARN THE RULES

You cannot edit confidently if you do not know the rules. Many people think the grammar and usage rules are understood only by English teachers, but the truth is that anyone can learn them. Invest in a grammar book, and each time you make an error, study the appropriate rule so that mistake does not happen again.

GET SOME HELP

Professional writers have editors who locate and correct errors that get by them, and you can get some help too. Ask someone to go over your writing to find mistakes that you overlooked. Be sure, however, that the person who helps you edit is someone who knows grammar and usage rules; otherwise, you will not get reliable information. If your school has a writing center, you may be able to stop in there for reliable editing assistance. Please keep in mind, though, that the ultimate responsibility for editing is yours. You must learn and apply the rules on your own, with only backup help from others.

USE A COMPUTER

The following techniques may help you edit with your computer.

Put your editing checklist into a window.   If your program allows you to split your screen, try placing your editing checklist (either the one on page 100 or one you devise) into a window. Consult the checklist as you edit.

Quadruple-space your text.   After revising, reformat your text with four spaces between each line. This way, you can edit one line at a time with less of your text entering your visual field to distract you from the words you are studying.

Edit the screen and the typed copy.   Edit twice. The first time through, edit by studying the words on the screen, making the necessary changes as you go. Then print your text and edit a second time on the paper copy. Enter these changes into your file and print a fresh copy.

Use the computer's search function to locate trouble spots.   For example, if you habitually misuse semicolons and confuse *to* and *too,* find every semicolon, *to,* and *too* in your draft and check your usage.

Use your computer's grammar check.   If your word processing program has a grammar check, use it to locate errors. Keep in mind, however, that these grammar checks are not foolproof. Therefore, you must carefully edit on your own.

"I Used a Period and a Capital Letter, so Why Isn't This a Sentence?"

From our earliest years in school, we have been taught to mark the start of a sentence with a capital letter and the end of a sentence with a period, question mark, or exclamation point. However, sometimes we carry that advice too far: We take a *piece* of a sentence, add a capital, place a period, and call what we get a whole sentence. However, a piece of a sentence (even with a capital letter and period added) is still just a *piece*—it is not a whole sentence. Instead, it is a sentence *fragment.* Here is an example of a sentence followed by a fragment:

Sentence
fragment: Maria has many admirable traits. Such as loyalty, creativity, and integrity.

Explanation: Despite the period and capital, *such as loyalty, creativity, and integrity* is only a piece of a sentence and does not have sentence status.

Fragment
eliminated: Maria has many admirable traits, such as loyalty, creativity, and integrity.

Explanation: The fragment is eliminated by joining it to the sentence.

If you have trouble editing for sentence fragments, the tips in the rest of this chapter should help you.

ISOLATE EVERYTHING YOU ARE CALLING A SENTENCE

Start at the beginning of your draft and place one finger of your left hand under the capital letter. Then place a finger of your right hand under the period, question mark, or exclamation point. Now read the word group between your fingers out loud. Does it sound as if something is missing? If not, you probably have a legitimate sentence. If so, then you probably have a sentence fragment.

Move through your entire draft this way, isolating word groups with your fingers and reading out loud. Each time you hear a fragment, stop and make the necessary correction. This procedure is time-consuming, but the payoff is worth the investment of time.

READ YOUR DRAFT BACKWARD

A good way to find fragments is to read your draft backward. Simply begin by reading the last sentence; pause for a moment to hear if something is missing, and then read the next-to-the-last sentence, again pausing to listen for something missing. Proceed this way until you have worked back to the first sentence. Each time you hear that something is missing, stop and correct the fragment you have found.

CHECK <u>-ING</u> AND <u>-ED</u> VERB FORMS

Sometimes sentence fragments result when *-ing* or *-ed* verb forms stand by themselves. Here are two examples with the *-ing* and *-ed* verb forms underlined.

Fragment: The kitten <u>stretching</u> after her nap.

Fragment: The child <u>frustrated</u> by the complicated toy.

To correct fragments that result when *-ing* or *-ed* verbs stand alone, pick an appropriate verb from this list and add it to the *-ing* or *-ed* form:

is	was	have	had
are	were	has	

Fragment: The kittens <u>stretching</u> after their naps.
Sentence: The kittens <u>are stretching</u> after their naps.
Sentence: The kittens <u>were stretching</u> after their naps.
Fragment: The child <u>frustrated</u> by the complicated toy.
Sentence: The child <u>is frustrated</u> by the complicated toy.
Sentence: The child <u>was frustrated</u> by the complicated toy.

To find fragments that result when *-ing* or *-ed* verbs stand alone, go through your draft checking each *-ing* and *-ed* verb form. Read the sentence with the form and ask if a verb from the above list is necessary for a sense of completeness.

CHECK FOR FRAGMENT WARNING WORDS

The following words often begin sentence fragments:

after	before	such as
although	especially	unless
as	even though	until
as if	for example	when
as long as	if	whenever
as soon as	in order to	where
as though	since	wherever
because	so that	while

Read aloud every word group that begins with one of the above words or phrases and listen carefully to hear if something is missing. Do not assume that anything beginning with one of these fragment warning words is automatically a sentence fragment because sentences, too, can begin with these words and phrases. To be sure, read aloud to hear if something is missing.

Sentence: While Rudy cleaned the house, Sue cooked dinner. (When you read these words out loud, there is no sense that something is missing.)

Fragment: While Rudy cleaned the house. (When you read these words out loud, you can hear that something is missing.)

WATCH OUT FOR WHO, WHOM, WHOSE, WHICH, AND WHERE

If you begin a word group with *who, whom, whose, which,* or *where* without asking a question, you have most likely written a sentence fragment.

Sentence: Who lives next door?

Fragment: Who lives next door.

Sentence: Whose advice have I valued over the years?

Fragment: Whose advice I have valued over the years.

Look at any word group that begins with *who, whom, whose, which,* or *where* and be sure that word group is asking a question. If it is not, join the word group to the sentence before it, as illustrated here:

Sentence
and fragment: Stavros is a good friend. Whose advice I have valued over the years.

Sentence: Stavros is a good friend, whose advice I have valued over the years.

ELIMINATE THE FRAGMENTS

The above techniques will help you locate sentence fragments; the next two techniques will help you eliminate fragments once you find them. Keep in mind, however, that no technique will work for every fragment, so if one correction method does not work, try the other.

Join the Fragment to a Sentence before or after It

Sentence and fragment:	The custom of hat-tipping goes back to the knights. <u>Who</u> would remove their helmets before a lord.
Fragment joined to sentence:	The custom of hat-tipping goes back to the knights, who would remove their helmets before a lord.
Fragment and sentence:	<u>While trying on the cashmere sweater.</u> Molly snagged the sleeve with her class ring.
Fragment joined to sentence:	While trying on the cashmere sweater, Molly snagged the sleeve with her class ring.

Add the Missing Word or Words

To eliminate a fragment that results when a word or words are left out (usually the subject or part of the verb), add the missing word or words.

Sentence and fragment:	The auto mechanic assured us the repairs would be minor. <u>Then proceeded to list a dozen things wrong with the car.</u>
Fragment eliminated with addition of the subject *he:*	The auto mechanic assured us the repairs would be minor. Then he proceeded to list a dozen things wrong with the car.
Fragment:	The Surgeon General announcing new nutritional guidelines.
Fragment eliminated with the addition of part of the verb *is:*	The Surgeon General is announcing new nutritional guidelines.
Sentence and fragment:	Police chiefs want to hire more officers. <u>However, not without additional funds.</u>

Fragment eliminated
with addition of
subject and verb:

`Police chiefs want to hire more officers.`
`However, they cannot do so without addi-`
`tional funds.`

USE A COMPUTER

Insert eight spaces before each capital letter that marks the start of a sentence. Then read each word group separately to hear if something is missing. Because each word group is now physically separated, finding fragments can be easier. When you are done with this aspect of editing, reformat your text to draw everything back together.

CHAPTER 17

"How Can This Be a Run-On or a Comma Splice? It's Not Even Long."

If you have a tendency to write run-on sentences or comma splices, take comfort in the fact that you are not alone. They are two of the most frequently occurring writing errors.

A *run-on sentence* occurs when two word groups that can be sentences (*independent clauses*) stand together without any separation. A *comma splice* occurs when two word groups that can be sentences (independent clauses) stand together with only a comma between them.

Here are two word groups that can be sentences (independent clauses):

Independent clause: Charleston Harbor is a fascinating place to visit

Independent clause: many historical attractions are there

A *run-on sentence* is created when these independent clauses are not separated:

Run-on sentence: Charleston Harbor is a fascinating place to visit many historical attractions are there.

109

A *comma splice* is created when two independent clauses are separated by nothing more than a comma:

Comma splice: Charleston Harbor is a fascinating place to visit, many historical attractions are there.

To eliminate run-on sentences and comma splices, the independent clauses can be separated in one of three ways, as follows:

1. **With a comma and coordinating conjunction (<u>and</u>, <u>but</u>, <u>or</u>, <u>nor</u>, <u>for</u>, <u>so</u>, <u>yet</u>)**

   Charleston Harbor is a fascinating place to visit<u>, for</u> many historical attractions are there.

2. **With a semicolon (;)**

   Charleston Harbor is a fascinating place to visi<u>t;</u> many historical attractions are there.

3. **With a period and a capital letter**

   Charleston Harbor is a fascinating place to visi<u>t. M</u>any historical attractions are there.

☞ *Be Careful:*   *Remember, a run-on sentence or comma splice occurs when you do not separate independent clauses in one of the above three ways.*

The rest of this chapter describes ways to find run-on sentences and comma splices in your writing.

STUDY SENTENCES INDIVIDUALLY

One way to find run-ons and comma splices is to study each of your sentences separately. Place one finger of your left hand under the capital letter and one finger of your right hand under the period, question mark, or exclamation point. Then identify the number of independent clauses (word groups that can stand as sentences) between your fingers. If you have one, the sentence is fine. If you have two or more, look to see what is separating the clauses. If a semicolon separates the independent clauses, the sentence is fine; if a comma and coordinating conjunction *(and, but, or, nor, for, so, yet)* separate the independent clauses, the sentence is fine. However, if nothing separates the independent clauses, or if only a comma without a coordinating conjunction separates the independent clauses, then you have a problem.

As mentioned previously, when you identify a run-on or comma splice, you can eliminate it by separating the independent clauses in one of three ways:

1. With a comma and a coordinating conjunction

2. With a semicolon

3. With a period and a capital letter

See page 110 for examples.

Move through your whole draft this way checking for and eliminating run-ons and comma splices. Although time-consuming, this procedure is very effective.

UNDERLINE RUN-ON AND COMMA SPLICE WARNING WORDS

When you edit for run-ons and comma splices, pay special attention to these words:

he	however	then	moreover	nevertheless
she	therefore	thus	furthermore	similarly
it	hence	finally	consequently	next
they	as a result	in addition	on the contrary	for example

Read over your draft and underline any of these warning words that appear. Then check to see what is on *both sides* of each underlined word. If an independent clause (a word group that can be a sentence) is on *both sides,* place a semicolon (not a comma) before the warning word.

FORGET ABOUT LONG AND SHORT

Many people think that a long sentence is sure to be a run-on or comma splice. Similarly, they think that a short sentence cannot possibly be one. This thinking is mistaken, for length is not a factor. The only factor is how independent clauses are separated, so during this phase of editing forget about how long or short your sentences are.

USE A COMPUTER

The strategies that follow will help you locate run-on sentences and comma splices using computer technology.

Search for warning words.   One way to edit for run-ons with a computer is to use the search function to find all the run-on warning words (see page 111). Once these words are identified in your text, check for independent clauses on both sides of these words. Wherever you find independent clauses on *both sides* of a warning word, be sure you have a semicolon before the word.

Isolate sentences.   Insert eight spaces before every capital letter marking the beginning of a sentence. This will visually separate your sentences from each other, making it easier to study sentences individually, following the procedure described on page 110. After finding and eliminating run-ons and comma splices, reformat your text to bring everything back together.

CHAPTER

18

"I/Me, She/Her, He/Him, They/Them, We/Us, Who/Whom—What's the Difference?"

There you are writing along merrily, and then it happens—you have to use a pronoun and you are not sure which one is correct: Did the police officer issue the warning to Lee and me or to Lee and I? "Lee and me; no, it's Lee and I; no, wait, Lee and me." Ah, what the heck—you pick one and hope for the best.

Writers often stumble over pronouns, but the procedures in this chapter can help.

CROSS OUT EVERYTHING IN THE PHRASE BUT THE PRONOUN

When a pronoun is linked with a noun, you may not be sure which pronoun to use. Is it "Luis and I" or "Luis and me"? Is it "the girls and us" or "the girls and we"? When in doubt, cross out everything in the phrase but the pronoun and read what is left:

~~My brothers and~~ I saw Batman six times.

~~My brothers and~~ me saw Batman six times.

With everything but the pronoun crossed out, you can tell that the correct choice is *I*:

```
My brothers and I saw Batman six times.
```

Here is another example:

```
Dr. Cohen lent Maria and I a copy of the book.
Dr. Cohen lent Maria and me a copy of the book.
```

With everything but the pronoun crossed out, you can tell that the correct choice is *me:*

```
Dr. Cohen lent Maria and me a copy of the book.
```

CROSS OUT WORDS THAT RENAME

Sometimes words follow a pronoun and rename it. The words that rename are called *appositives.*

We baseball players:	*Baseball players* follows the pronoun and renames it.
Us sophomores:	*Sophomores* follows the pronoun and renames it.
You sports fans:	*Sports fans* follows the pronoun and renames it.

To make pronoun choice easier, cross out the words that rename (the appositives):

```
We spectators jumped to our feet and cheered when the band
took the field.
Us spectators jumped to our feet and cheered when the band
took the field.
```

With the appositive crossed out, the correct choice is clear:

```
We spectators jumped to our feet and cheered when the band
took the field.
```

Here is another example:

```
Loud rock music can be irritating to we ~~older folks~~.
Loud rock music can be irritating to us ~~older folks~~.
```

With the appositive crossed out, the correct choice is clear:

```
Loud rock music can be irritating to us older folks.
```

ADD THE MISSING WORDS IN COMPARISONS

Which is it: "Bev is a better foul shooter than I" or "Bev is a better foul shooter than me"? To find out, add the unstated comparison word:

```
Bev is a better foul shooter than I am.
Bev is a better foul shooter than me am.
```

With the missing word added, you can tell that the correct pronoun is *I:*

```
Bev is a better foul shooter than I.
```

Here is another example:

```
John Jakes's new novel interested Miguel as much as I.
John Jakes's new novel interested Miguel as much as me.
```

To decide on the correct pronoun, add the missing words:

```
John Jakes's new novel interested Miguel as much as it in-
terested I.
John Jakes's new novel interested Miguel as much as it in-
terested me.
```

With the missing comparison words added, you can tell that the correct pronoun is *me.*

CIRCLE <u>THEY</u>, <u>THEIR</u>, AND <u>THEM</u>, AND DRAW AN ARROW TO THE NOUNS THEY REFER TO

They, their, and *them* refer to plural nouns:

```
All students should bring (their) notebooks to the next
class; if (they) forget (them), class participation will prove
difficult.
```

A problem occurs when *they, their,* or *them* is used to refer to a singular noun:

```
A person who cares about the environment will recycle.
(They) will also avoid using Styrofoam and plastic.
```

In the previous sentence the plural *they* refers to the singular *person.* This creates a problem called *lack of agreement.* To eliminate this problem, make the pronoun and noun agree in one of these two ways:

Singular noun
and pronoun:
```
A person who cares about the environment will
recycle. (He or she) will also avoid using Sty-
rofoam and plastic.
```

Plural noun
and pronoun:
```
People who care about the environment will re-
cycle. (They) will also avoid using Styrofoam
and plastic.
```

One way to ensure agreement is to circle *they, their,* and *them* and then draw arrows to the nouns referred to. Be sure each of these pronouns refers to a plural noun. If it does not, make the noun plural or change the pronoun to a singular form.

PAY SPECIAL ATTENTION TO <u>EVERYBODY</u>, <u>EVERYONE</u>, <u>EVERYTHING</u>, <u>SOMEBODY</u>, <u>SOMEONE</u>, <u>SOMETHING</u>, <u>ANYBODY</u>, <u>ANYONE</u>, AND <u>ANYTHING</u>

In formal usage, these nine words (called *indefinite pronouns*) are singular (*-body, -one,* and *-thing* at the end can help you remember this). Thus, pronouns that refer to these words should also be singular if you are writing for an audience that expects formal usage. Here are some examples:

Everybody should remember <u>his or her</u> admission forms when reporting to orientation.

Someone left <u>his or her</u> coat in the auditorium.

Anybody who wants to bring <u>his or her</u> family may do so.

Be sure to put everything in <u>its</u> place.

When you edit, look for these nine words. If you find one, look to see if a pronoun refers to it. If so, be sure that the pronoun is singular. Do not rely on the sound of the sentence because the plural pronoun may sound fine since it is often used in informal spoken English.

CIRCLE <u>WHO</u> AND <u>WHOM</u> AND UNDERLINE THE REST OF THE CLAUSE

Writers often have trouble choosing between *who* and *whom*. To solve the problem, circle *who* or *whom* and underline the rest of the clause (word group with a subject and verb). If the circled word acts as a subject, use *who*. If it is the object, use *whom*. Here are some examples:

Hippocrates, (who or whom?) lived about 400 B.C., is called the "Father of Medicine."

Choose *who* because it is the subject of the verb *lived*.

Hippocrates, who lived about 400 B.C., is called the "Father of Medicine."

I attended the lecture by the Holocaust survivor (who or whom?) the community invited to speak.

Choose *whom* because it is the object of the verb *invited*.

I attended the lecture by the Holocaust survivor whom the community invited to speak.

CIRCLE <u>YOU</u>

The pronoun *you* addresses the reader; if it is used to refer to someone other than the reader, the result is a problem called *person shift*. To avoid this problem, circle *you* and draw an arrow to the word it refers to. If this word names someone other than the reader, replace *you* with the correct pronoun. Here is an example:

```
Distance runners must train religiously. (You) cannot com-
pete successfully if (you) run only on weekends.
```

Now here is the corrected version:

```
Distance runners must train religiously. (They) cannot com-
pete successfully if (they) run only on weekends.
```

UNDERLINE IT AND THEY TO AVOID UNSTATED REFERENCE

Underline *it* and *they* and then check to be sure you have supplied a noun for these words to refer to. Otherwise, you will have a problem called *unstated reference.*

Unstated reference:	Charlie is a very curious child. Because of <u>it</u>, he asks questions all the time.
Explanation:	*It* cannot refer to *curious* because *curious* is a modifier, not a noun. The reference is meant to be *curiosity,* but that word is not stated.
Correction:	Charlie is a very curious child. Because of his curiosity, he asks questions all the time.
Unstated reference:	When I went to the unemployment office, <u>they</u> told me that some construction jobs were available.
Explanation:	There is no stated noun for *they* to refer to.
Correction:	When I went to the unemployment office, the employment counselor told me that some construction jobs were available.

WATCH OUT FOR UNCLEAR REFERENCE

When a pronoun can refer to more than one noun and the reader cannot tell what the writer means, the problem is *unclear reference.*

Unclear reference:	Dad was in the garage with Brian when he heard the telephone ring.
Explanation:	Because of unclear reference, the reader can't tell whether Dad or Brian heard the phone.
Correction:	Dad was in the garage with Brian when Brian heard the telephone ring.

USE A COMPUTER

The search function of your word processing program can help you check your use of some pronouns. First, use the search function to locate these pronouns in your draft: *they, their, them.* Then check to be sure that you have plural nouns for these words to refer to. Also, check to be sure *they* has a stated noun to refer to.

Next, use the search function to locate every use of *everyone, everybody, everything, someone, somebody, something, anyone, anybody,* and *anything.* Check to see if a pronoun refers to each of these words. If so, use the singular form for formal usage.

Now use the search function to locate every use of *who* and *whom.* If the word is used as a subject, use *who;* if it is used as an object, use *whom.*

Finally, use your search function to locate every use of *you.* Then see if you need to change this pronoun because it is not really referring to the reader.

"I'm Not Sure Which Verb to Use."

A student once joked that she knows why verbs are called "action words"—because they so *actively* cause her trouble. Choosing the right verb *can* be tricky at times, but most of the problems arise in just a few special instances. Strategies for dealing with these instances are discussed in this chapter.

CROSS OUT PHRASES BEFORE THE VERB

A phrase before the verb can trick you into choosing the wrong verb form. Consider this sentence:

    The stack of books (is or are?) about to fall.

Is it *The stack is* or *The books are*? To decide, cross out the phrase *of books* to get:

    The stack ~~of books~~ is about to fall.

Phrases before the verb often begin with one of these words (called *prepositions*):

about	before	inside	over
above	between	into	through
across	by	like	to
after	during	near	toward
among	for	next	under
around	from	of	up
at	in	on	with

When in doubt about the correct verb form, cross out phrases beginning with one of these words. Here are some examples:

```
The container of old dishes (is or are?) on the landing.
The container of old dishes (is or are?) on the landing.
The container of old dishes is on the landing.
```

```
The herd of steers (graze or grazes?) contentedly.
The herd of steers (graze or grazes?) contentedly.
The herd of steers grazes contentedly.
```

```
The characteristics of the German shepherd (make or
makes?) him a suitable show dog.
The characteristics of the German shepherd (make or
makes?) him a suitable show dog.
The characteristics of the German shepherd make him a suit-
able show dog.
```

REWRITE QUESTIONS

Choosing the correct verb form can be tricky in sentences that ask questions, because the verb comes before the subject. Verb choice becomes much easier, however, if you rewrite the sentence so it is no longer a question. Here is an example:

Sentence with
question: (<u>Have</u> or <u>has</u>?) the students finished taking exams?

Sentence
rewritten: The students have finished taking exams.

Sentence with
question and
correct verb: Have the students finished taking exams?

REWRITE SENTENCES BEGINNING WITH <u>HERE</u> AND <u>THERE</u>

When a sentence begins with *here* or *there,* the verb comes before the subject, which can make choosing the correct verb a little tricky. To be sure you have the correct verb, rewrite the sentence putting the subject before the verb. The correct choice should be easier that way.

Sentence
with *here:* Here (<u>is</u> or <u>are</u>?) the important papers you asked for.

Sentence
rewritten: The important papers you asked for are here.

Sentence
with *here*
and correct
verb: Here are the important papers you asked for.

Sentence
with *there:* There (<u>was</u> or <u>were</u>?) an excellent dance band playing at the wedding reception.

Sentence
rewritten: An excellent dance band was playing at the wedding reception.

Sentence
with *there*
and correct
verb: There was an excellent dance band playing at the wedding reception.

CIRCLE EACH, EITHER, NEITHER, ONE, NONE, ANYONE, ANYBODY, ANYTHING, EVERYONE, EVERYBODY, EVERYTHING, SOMEONE, SOMEBODY, AND SOMETHING

These words are *indefinite pronouns,* and in formal usage they take singular verbs—even though the sense of the sentence suggests that a plural verb is logical. To check for the correct verb when you have used one of these words as the subject of a sentence, circle the word and draw an arrow to the verb. Then check that verb to be sure it is singular.

(Each) of the students wants (not <u>want</u>) to have the test on Friday so the weekend is more relaxing.

(One) of the first museums was (not <u>were</u>) Altes Museum in Berlin.

(Either) of these vacation plans meets (not <u>meet</u>) your needs.

(Neither) of these paintings suits (not <u>suit</u>) my taste.

(None) of Lin's excuses is (not <u>are</u>) believable.

Do not rely on the sound of the sentence with these words because the plural verb may sound just fine, and the singular verb may sound a little off. This is because the plural verb is often used in informal speech and writing. Nonetheless, use the singular verb for strict grammatical correctness in formal usage.

LISTEN TO YOUR VERB TENSES

Tense means time. Many verbs change their form to show different tenses (times):

Present tense
(time):   Today I <u>walk</u> two miles for exercise.

Past tense
(time):   Yesterday I <u>walked</u> two miles for exercise.

Future tense
(time):   Tomorrow I <u>will walk</u> two miles for exercise.

Sometimes a change in verb tense is necessary to show a change in time, but sometimes writers change tense inappropriately and create a problem called *tense shift.*

Appropriate change
in tense from
present to past: I <u>recall</u> that April Fools' Day <u>began</u> in
France.

Problem tense shift
from present to past: After I <u>finish</u> my work, I <u>watched</u> a movie.

If you have a tendency to write inappropriate tense shifts, read your draft out loud and listen to your verb tenses. You are likely to hear problem shifts if you are careful to read exactly what is on the page.

"I Have Trouble with the Forms of Modifiers."

A *modifier* is a word or phrase that describes a word. For example, consider this sentence:

> Because of the accident, traffic moved slowly.

Because *slowly* describes *moved, slowly* is a modifier. Modifiers take different forms in different grammatical settings, and if those forms give you some trouble, the suggestions in this chapter can help.

DRAW AN ARROW FROM THE MODIFIER TO THE WORD DESCRIBED

Which sentence is correct?

> The party ended so <u>quickly</u> that no one had a chance to eat.

> The party ended so <u>quick</u> that no one had a chance to eat.

If you are unsure, you may have trouble knowing when to use adjectives and when to use adverbs. An *adjective* describes a noun or pronoun, and an *adverb* describes a verb or other modifier. Frequently, the adverb form ends in *-ly* and the adjective form does not.

Adjectives	Adverbs
brief	briefly
swift	swiftly
loud	loudly
clear	clearly

If you are unsure which form to use, draw an arrow from the modifier to the word it describes. If the arrow is drawn to a noun or pronoun, then use the adjective form. If the arrow is drawn to a verb or modifier, then use the adverb form. Here is an example.

Is it *quick* or *quickly* in this sentence?

```
Diane mowed the lawn (quick or quickly?) so she could leave
with her friends.
```

To decide, draw an arrow from the modifier to the word described. If the word described is a noun or a pronoun, use the adjective; if it is a verb or another modifier, use the adverb (which often ends in *-ly*).

```
Diane mowed the lawn (quick or quickly?) so she could
leave with her friends.
```

Now you can tell that *quickly* is called for because a verb is described:

```
Diane mowed the lawn quickly so she could leave with her
friends.
```

Here are some more examples:

```
David was (absolute or absolutely?) sure of the answer.
```
David was absolutely sure of the answer. (A modifier is described, so the adverb is used.)

```
The ancient Egyptians thought of the soul as a bird that
could fly around (easy or easily?).
```
The ancient Egyptians thought of the soul as a bird that could fly around easily. (A verb is described, so the adverb is used.)

Chris felt (happy or happily?) that he was promoted after only one month on the job.

Chris felt happy that he was promoted after only one month on the job. (A noun is described, so the adjective is used.)

REMEMBER THAT <u>GOOD</u> IS AN ADJECTIVE AND <u>WELL</u> IS AN ADVERB—WITH ONE CAUTION AND ONE EXCEPTION

Good is an adjective; it describes nouns and pronouns:

The good news is that I got the job.

Well is an adverb; it describes verbs and modifiers:

After ten years of lessons, Maxine plays the piano well.

☞ *Note: Now here's the caution:*

After verbs like *taste, seem, appear,* and *look,* use *good* because the noun or pronoun before the verb is being described.

The meat tastes good, even though it is overcooked.
Claudia's appearance looks good, although she just had surgery.
The restaurant seems good, so let's eat here.

☞ *Note: Now here's the exception:*

Well is used as an adjective to mean "in good health."

After six brownies and a bottle of soda, the child did not feel well.

EACH TIME YOU USE <u>MORE</u> OR <u>MOST</u>, CHECK TO BE SURE YOU HAVE NOT USED AN <u>-ER</u> OR <u>-EST</u> FORM

Yes: I like tacos <u>better</u> than nachos.
No: I like tacos <u>more better</u> than nachos.

Yes: The Sahara Desert is the world's <u>hottest</u> region in summer.

No: The Sahara Desert is the world's <u>most hottest</u> region in summer.

Yes: The Sahara Desert is <u>bigger</u> than the United States.

No: The Sahara Desert is <u>more bigger</u> than the United States.

Yes: The <u>rainiest</u> place on earth is Mount Waialeale, in Hawaii.

No: The <u>most rainiest</u> place on earth is Mount Waialeale, in Hawaii.

CHECK EVERY SENTENCE THAT OPENS WITH AN <u>-ING</u> OR <u>-ED</u> VERB FORM

An *-ing* or *-ed* verb form can be used as an adjective:

Whistling, Carolyn strolled through the park.

Whistling is a verb form that is used as an adjective to describe *Carolyn*.

Living only two or three years, lizards have a short life span.

Living is a verb form used as an adjective to describe *lizards.*

When an *-ing* or *-ed* form opens a sentence, it should be followed by the word that the form describes. Otherwise, the result will be a *dangling modifier.* Dangling modifiers can create some pretty silly sentences:

Dangling modifier: While making the coffee, the toast burned. (This sentence says that the toast made the coffee.)

Correction: While making the coffee, I burned the toast. (The opening *-ing* verb form is followed by a word it can sensibly describe.)

Dangling modifier: Exhausted from work, a nap was needed. (This sentence says that the nap was exhausted.)

Correction:	Exhausted from work, Lucy needed a nap. (The opening *-ed* verb form is followed by a word it can logically describe.)

If you are in the habit of writing dangling modifiers, check every opening *-ing* and *-ed* verb form and be sure it is closely followed by a word it can sensibly describe.

MOVE MODIFIERS NEAR THE WORDS THEY DESCRIBE

If a modifier is too far from the word it describes, the result is known as a *misplaced modifier*. A misplaced modifier can create a silly sentence:

Misplaced modifier:	Lee bought a bicycle from a neighbor with a flat tire. (The sentence says that the neighbor had a flat tire.)
Correction:	Lee bought a bicycle with a flat tire from a neighbor. (The modifier has been moved closer to the word it describes.)

"Why Can't I Place
a Comma Wherever
I Pause?"

Placing commas wherever you pause is not a reliable method of punctuating: sometimes it works and sometimes it does not. If you are unsure about when to use commas, learn the rules. Until you do, the techniques in this chapter will help you identify some—but not all—of the occasions when you need commas.

FIND THE SUBJECT AND LOOK IN FRONT OF IT

Most of the time, anything that comes before the subject of a sentence is set off with a comma. It does not matter whether the material is a single word, a phrase, or a clause. Thus, once you identify the subject of a sentence, you can look in front of it. If there are any words there, follow them with a comma, like this:

Word before
the subject:

subject
Surprisingly, [the heart of a whale] beats only nine times a minute.

130

Phrase before
the subject:

subject

In medieval Japan, [fashionable women] black-
ened their teeth to enhance their appearance.

Clause before
the subject:

Although Albert Einstein developed the theory
subject
of relativity, [he] failed his first college en-
trance exam.

CIRCLE <u>AND</u>, <u>BUT</u>, <u>OR</u>, <u>NOR</u>, <u>FOR</u>, <u>SO</u>, <u>YET</u> AND LOOK LEFT AND RIGHT

If a word group that can stand as a sentence (an *independent clause*) appears on *both sides* of *and, but, or, nor, for, so, yet (coordinating conjunctions),* you should place a comma before the conjunction.

To apply this rule, circle every coordinating conjunction; then look left and right. If an independent clause appears on both sides, place a comma before the conjunction.

Use comma:

independent clause

[I enjoy reading Stephen King novels], (but) [I do
independent clause
not enjoy watching horror movies.]

Use comma:

independent clause

[The Centers for Disease Control predicts a flu
independent clause
outbreak], (so) [I plan to get a flu shot.]

Use comma:

independent clause

[Fish can distinguish colors], (and) [they actu-
independent clause
ally prefer some colors over others.]

Do not
use comma:

The owl has no motion in its eyes (but) [can turn
not a clause
its head around.]

Do not
use comma:

not a clause

The car accelerated quickly (and) [turned left.]

Do not
use comma:

not a clause

You can leave with me now (or) [wait until later.]

LOOK FOR SERIES

A *series* is three or more words, phrases, or clauses. Each time you find a series in your writing, separate the items in that series with commas.

Words in a series:	This restaurant specializes in <u>pasta</u>, <u>steak</u>, <u>salads</u>, and <u>seafood</u>.
Phrases in a series:	Recycling centers have been established <u>at the government center</u>, <u>behind the high school</u>, and <u>at the baseball fields</u>.
Clauses in a series:	<u>The manager lowered prices</u>, <u>the sales staff tried to be more helpful</u>, and <u>the owner remodeled the store</u>.

IDENTIFY NONESSENTIAL ELEMENTS

A *nonessential element* can be removed without changing the meaning of the sentence. Identify nonessential elements and set them off with commas. In the following sentences, the nonessential elements are underscored as a study aid.

Nonessential word:	The president at the time, <u>Carter</u>, worked to achieve the Egyptian-Israeli peace agreement.
Nonessential word:	The governor, <u>surprisingly</u>, opposed the balanced-budget amendment.
Nonessential phrase:	You can, <u>of course</u>, join us for dinner.
Nonessential phrase:	The crime rate, <u>according to the newsletter</u>, has not increased this year.
Nonessential clause:	Very few people understand how the election process works, <u>if you ask me</u>.
Nonessential clause:	Karen Carpenter, <u>who died of anorexia nervosa</u>, was a talented performer.

"I Have Trouble with Apostrophes."

Apostrophes have two main functions: They are used in contractions to take the place of missing letters, and they signal possession. Some people think apostrophes have a third function: to drive them crazy. Apostrophes *can* be pesky, so if you are unsure how to use them, try the techniques presented in this chapter.

IDENTIFY THE MISSING LETTER(S)

In contractions, discover which letter or letters are missing, and place the apostrophe at the site of the missing letter(s). For example, the contraction form of *did not* is *didn't*. Because the *o* is left out of *not,* the apostrophe is placed between the *n* and the *t.* Here are some more examples:

  have + not = haven't (apostrophe at site of missing *o*)

  we + will = we'll (apostrophe at site of missing *wi*)

it + is = it's (apostrophe at site of missing *i*)

☞ *Note: The contraction form of will not is the unusual won't.*

USE IT'S ONLY WHEN YOU CAN SUBSTITUTE IT IS OR IT HAS

1. It's is the contraction form of it is or it has.

It's time for a change of leadership in this state.
(It is time for a change of leadership in this state.)

It's been ten years since I smoked a cigarette.
(It has been ten years since I smoked a cigarette.)

2. Its is a possessive form; it shows ownership and cannot be substituted for it is or it has.

Yes: The river overflowed its banks. (*Its* shows ownership.)

No: Its too late to turn back now.

Yes: It's too late to turn back now. (*It's* here means *it is*.)

AVOID CONTRACTIONS

No law says that you must use contractions. If you are unsure where to place the apostrophe, use the two-word form instead of the one-word contraction.

FOR POSSESSIVE FORMS, ASK TWO QUESTIONS

Apostrophes are used with nouns to show possession. To determine how to use the apostrophe, ask, "Does the noun end in *s*?"

1. If the noun does not end in s, add an apostrophe and an s, like this:

President + 's = President's

The President's Council on Aging reports an increase in homelessness among the elderly.

children + 's = children's

Children's toys cost more money than they are worth.

2. If the noun ends in s̲, ask, "Is the noun singular or plural?"

a. If the noun is singular, add an apostrophe and an s̲, like this:

Delores + 's = Delores's

Delores's new car was hit in the parking lot.

bus + 's = bus's

The bus's brakes jammed, causing a minor accident.

b. If the noun is plural, add an apostrophe, like this:

shoes + ' = shoes'

All the shoes' laces are too long.

mayors + ' = mayors'

The three mayors' mutual aid agreement is sure to yield economic benefits.

USE A COMPUTER

If you use your computer's spell checker, keep in mind that many programs do not check apostrophes in contractions. This means that misspellings such as "cant" will not be noted.

CHAPTER

23

"I Can't Spell."

There's good news and bad news. First the bad news: Misspelled words are a real problem because they lead the reader to think you are not very capable. Now the good news: Lots of very capable people do not spell well, but they have learned ways to solve their spelling problem. You, too, can eliminate misspellings if you use the techniques in this chapter.

WHEN IN DOUBT, CHECK IT OUT

When it comes to using a dictionary, we all get lazy. Still, the only surefire way to check a spelling is to look up the word. If you have even the slightest suspicion that a word is misspelled, check the dictionary. Remember, it does not matter how many words you misspell, as long as you correct the misspellings before your writing reaches your reader.

BUY TWO DICTIONARIES

So looking words up is as convenient as possible, invest in two dictionaries. Buy one hardback collegiate dictionary to keep on your writing desk and one fat paperback to carry with you. You are more likely to look up a word if you have a dictionary at hand and do not have to get up and walk somewhere to check a spelling.

USE A SPELLING DICTIONARY

Spelling dictionaries, available in most drugstores and bookstores, reference frequently misspelled words. They provide spellings without definitions, so these volumes are thin, which makes them convenient to carry around. If you must look up words often, a spelling dictionary may prove less cumbersome than a standard dictionary.

USE A POCKET SPELL CHECKER

Pocket spell checkers are electronic gadgets about the size of some calculators. They can be expensive, but if you are more inclined to check spellings with an electronic gizmo than with a dictionary, they are worth the money.

LEARN CORRECT PRONUNCIATIONS

Sometimes people misspell because they pronounce a word incorrectly. For example, *February* may be misspelled if it is pronounced "Feb · u · ary"; *preventive* may be misspelled if it is pronounced "pre · ven · ta · tive." Learning to pronounce words correctly is the first step in spelling them correctly.

BREAK A WORD INTO PARTS

When a word is composed of identifiable parts, spell the word out part by part. Words like the following may be more manageable when spelled out part by part:

under · stand · able	with · hold	arm · chair
room · mate	kinder · garten	dis · ease
comfort · able	lone · liness	over · coat

BREAK A WORD INTO SYLLABLES

Some words are more easily spelled if you go syllable by syllable. Words of three or more syllables are often better handled this way.

or · gan · i · za · tion	cit · i · zen	mon · u · men · tal
Jan · u · ar · y	in · vi · ta · tion	hos · pi · tal
in · di · vis · i · ble	con · ver · sa · tion	pro · ba · bly

LOOK FOR PREFIXES

When a prefix (word beginning) is added to a word, the spelling of the base word will probably not change.

mis · take	dis · satisfaction	mis · spell
un · nerve	un · necessary	pre · pare
mis · inform	inter · related	pre · record

USE MEMORY TRICKS

Think of tricks to help you spell words you have trouble with. For example, the word *instrument* contains *strum,* and you strum a guitar, which is an instrument. Actors in a *tragedy* often *rage* at each other.

Memory tricks can be particularly helpful for pairs of words that are often mistaken for each other. You may find some of the following tricks to your liking, and you may want to make up tricks for other pairs of words that you confuse.

1. **advice/advise**

   a. *Advice* means "a suggestion."

   Joel's <u>advice</u> proved sound.

b. *Advise* means "to give advice."

Yvette is the best person to advise you.

☞ *Memory Trick: A person with a <u>vice</u> needs ad<u>vice</u>.*

2. affect/effect

a. *Affect* means "to influence."

The drought will affect the economy for years to come.

b. *Effect* means "result."

The effects of the drought are devastating.

☞ *Memory Trick: The first syllable of <u>effect</u> rhymes with the first syllable of <u>result</u>.*

3. all ready/already

a. *All ready* means "all set."

By three o'clock, the family was all ready to leave for Virginia Beach.

b. *Already* means "by this time."

We are already an hour behind schedule, and we haven't begun the trip yet.

☞ *Memory Trick: <u>All ready</u> and <u>all set</u> are two words.*

4. among/between

a. *Among* is used for more than two.

Divide the candy among the four children.

b. *Between* is used for two.

The difference between the ages of Phil and Carlos is not important.

☞ *Memory Trick: Can you fit anything <u>between</u> the <u>two e's</u> in the last syllable of <u>between</u>?*

5. beside/besides

a. *Beside* means "alongside of."

I parked the van beside the Corvette.

b. *Besides* means "in addition to."

Besides good soil, the plants need water.

☞ *Memory Trick: The final s in <u>besides</u> is "in addition to" the first s.*

6. fewer/less

    a. *Fewer* is for things that can be counted.

        <u>Fewer</u> people voted in this election than in the last one.

    b. *Less* is used for things that cannot be counted.

        People who exercise regularly experience <u>less</u> stress than those who do not.

☞ *Memory Trick: Think of <u>countless</u>. Less is used for things that cannot be counted.*

7. passed/past

    a. *Passed* means "went by" or "handed."

        Katie <u>passed</u> the potatoes to Earvin.
        The shooting star <u>passed</u> overhead at nine o'clock.

    b. *Past* refers to previous time. It also means "by."

        I have learned from <u>past</u> experience not to trust Jerry.
        When I drove <u>past</u> the house, no one was home.

☞ *Memory trick: Remember the <u>p</u> and <u>t</u> in <u>past</u> and <u>p</u>revious <u>t</u>ime.*

8. then/than

    a. *Then* refers to a certain time.

        The trumpets blared; <u>then</u> the cymbals crashed.

    b. *Than* is used to compare.

        I like small classes better <u>than</u> large lectures.

☞ *Memory Trick: Think of the <u>e</u> in <u>then</u> and <u>time</u>; think of the <u>a</u> in <u>than</u> and <u>compare</u>.*

UNDERLINE WORDS TO CHECK LATER

When you write a word while drafting or revising, you may have a sense that it is spelled wrong. Yet, looking the word up at that point is undesirable because it interrupts the drafting or revising momentum. Later you may forget to look up the word or no longer realize it may be misspelled, so it may remain incorrect. To solve this problem, underline every word whose spelling you are unsure of as you write it. Then you have a visual reminder to look up the word later, when it is more convenient.

KEEP A SPELLING LIST

People who are serious about improving their spelling often look up the words they misspell and add the words, correctly spelled, to a list for study. Each day, they study the list and memorize another word or two in an effort to increase the number of words they know how to spell.

USE A COMPUTER

Many word processing programs come with spell checkers. If yours does not, or if you desire a more powerful spell checker, you can purchase one as an add-on program.

Spell checkers test every word you have written against the words in the dictionary in the computer's memory. If a word is not recognized, the spell checker will offer alternative spellings. If the spell checker comes across a typing error, it may be baffled if nothing in its memory comes close to the spelling. In this case, it will not know what to suggest as a correct spelling. Also, homophones (soundalikes) are untouched by spell checkers, so the confusion of something like *there, their, they're* will not be resolved. Despite these limitations, spell checkers can be helpful to people with chronic spelling problems.

P A R T

Writing Practice

The writing tasks in the next chapter will give you opportunities to practice so you can continue to improve. If you get stuck along the way, refer to the appropriate chapters of this book for troubleshooting suggestions. But remember, the procedures described do not guarantee success; they are techniques you can try to ease the way. The only surefire way to improve is to keep writing and assessing your writing process.

CHAPTER

24

Ideas for Writing

1. The student services division of your university plans to publish a handbook for incoming freshmen to familiarize them with some of the most common procedures on campus. As a student employee in student services, you have been asked to contribute to the handbook by writing an essay that explains how to do one of the following:

   a. Check a book out of the library.

   b. Register for courses.

   c. Select a suitable advisor.

   d. Rush a fraternity or sorority.

   e. Manage stress.

   f. Study for final examinations.

   g. Find a compatible roommate.

   h. Make friends.

   i. Select a major.

   When you write the essay, remember that your audience will be new freshmen, your role will be that of an advisor, and your purpose will be to inform freshmen so they are better able to cope with campus life.

2. The administration of your university is very concerned about the amount of drinking on your campus and has begun a full-scale study to determine if students are drinking to excess and thereby endangering themselves. You are the president of the student council, and you have been directed to prepare a report that tells the percentage of students who are drinking, the extent of that drinking, the number of students who are underage drinkers, the kind of alcohol drunk, and where the drinking occurs. In addition, you can include any other information you think is pertinent, such as whether drinking is interfering with schoolwork and whether it is endangering students. Finally, include an alcohol policy you think the administration should adopt. This policy can include ways to educate students, how to discipline them for drinking, and so forth. Your audience will be the campus administration, your role will be that of knowledgeable student, and your purpose will be to inform the administration of the nature and extent of drinking on your campus from the students' point of view and to persuade them to adopt your policy. (If necessary, interview people on campus to get the information you need for your report.)

3. A big birthday bash is being planned for someone you respect and care a great deal for (pick anyone you regard highly—a friend, a relative, a teacher, a coach, a member of the clergy). You have been asked to write a character sketch of the person that presents and illustrates one or two of the person's best traits. Mention the trait or traits and go on to give examples that illustrate the trait(s). The sketch will be photocopied and distributed to everyone in attendance. Your audience will be people who also know and care for the person, your role will be that of an admirer, and your purpose will be to praise the person by sharing impressions and experiences.

4. You are a member of the local Chamber of Commerce, which is putting together a brochure to promote tourism in your area. Pick a spot in your area (a recreational spot, a historic area, an educational place, an amusement spot) and write a description of it to be included in the brochure. Your audience is the traveler looking for a place to spend some time, your purpose is to persuade the person to visit your area, and your role is that of someone who takes pride in the spot you are describing.

5. For the last week you have been home with the flu, and to pass the time you have watched a great deal of television. The programming

aimed at children, you have noticed, is mind-numbing. Even worse, the shows and accompanying commercials are manipulative, aimed at getting children to pester their parents for toys and sugared food. You become outraged and write a letter of protest to the networks. Your purpose is to persuade the networks to improve the quality of shows and commercials aimed at children, and your role is that of a concerned citizen.

6. When you were in high school, you were the editor of the school newspaper. Now your alma mater is planning a press day, and you have been asked to deliver a speech that expresses whether or not you believe high school principals should be permitted to censor the contents of high school publications. Your audience will be the newspaper and yearbook staffs; your purpose will be to persuade your audience to adopt your view; your role is that of a former high school journalist keenly interested in censorship issues. Before writing your speech, you may want to find recent newspaper and magazine articles on censorship of high school newspapers.

7. Congratulations! You are the winner of a writing contest. Your prize is the opportunity to have a 500- to 700-word essay published in the magazine of your choice. You may write on any topic and for any purpose. Just be sure your material is suitable for the readers of whatever magazine you choose.

8. Your campus newspaper is looking for guest columnists. Submit an article titled "Being a College Student Is Just Slightly Easier Than Eating Jell-O with a Butter Knife." Your audience is the university community, and your purpose is to entertain, using humor (make the piece funny). Your role is that of a slightly exasperated college student.

9. You have recently acquired a pen pal who lives in another country. He or she has asked that in each letter you describe a different facet of American life, as honestly and precisely as possible. Pick one aspect and write a thorough description for someone who knows very little about this country. Your purpose is to inform, and your role is that of an ambassador and teacher.

10. Pick a controversial issue you feel strongly about and write a letter to the editor of your town newspaper expressing your view on the issue. Your audience is the readers of the newspaper, your purpose is to persuade them to think or act in accordance with your view, and your role is that of a concerned citizen.

11. You are a member of the local school board. Recently, a number of parents have complained because commencement ceremonies

traditionally begin with a nondenominational prayer. Although no particular religion is represented by the prayer, these parents maintain that any prayer is inappropriate because it violates the separation of church and state guaranteed by the Constitution. Furthermore, these parents maintain that the rights of atheists are violated by the prayer. Do you support the view of these parents? Write a position paper that either recommends abolishing the prayer or recommends retaining it, and support your stand. Your audience is the rest of the school board, and your purpose is to convince them to take the course of action you recommend.

12. As part of a job application, you have been asked to write a character sketch of yourself that presents and illustrates your chief strengths and weaknesses. Your audience is the personnel director, your purpose is to present a realistic yet favorable portrait, and your role is that of job applicant.

13. If you have a job, assume that your boss has asked you to write a report that describes one change that could be made to improve efficiency, morale, or profitability. You are to explain the change, why it is needed, and how it would improve operations. Your audience is the chief management person, your purpose is to persuade this person to institute the change, and your role is that of a dedicated employee.

14. You are taking a study skills class, and your instructor has assigned a paper that requires you to classify and describe the study habits of students. To research this paper, interview as many students as necessary to discover how they study, how much they study, when they study, where they study, and so forth. Your audience is your instructor, your purpose is to inform, and your role is that of a student who wants to do well in the course.

15. You are taking a psychology course, and to help you appreciate how people are affected by events in their lives, your instructor has asked you to write an essay that explains how some event in your life has affected you (a death, a divorce, making a game-winning touchdown, being cut from a team, being class president, failing a test, moving to a new town, getting a speeding ticket, and so on). Your instructor has asked that you write the essay for someone you feel close to in order to share a significant part of your life. Your role is that of close friend or relative of your reader.

Appendixes

The sample process log in Appendix 1 offers a way to keep track of the procedures you use when you write and a way to assess the success of those procedures. This way you will know when to sample new procedures for a particular aspect of the process.

The sample reader response questionnaire in Appendix 2 offers a way to get the reactions of others to your drafts to help you decide what changes to make.

The tips for coping with essay examinations in Appendix 3 will help students perform successfully in pressure situations.

Keeping a Process Log

Becoming a better writer involves discovering writing procedures that work well. Throughout this book, you have read descriptions of many procedures. No doubt, some of them worked well for you, and some of them did not. Each time you write, you should be aware of what you do to handle idea generation, drafting, revising, and editing. You should assess which procedures were successful for you and which were not. That way, you can decide which procedures to incorporate into your writing process and which ones to replace.

Figure 3 shows a sample process log, which can help you identify your current writing process and ways to improve it. Fill out a log like this each time you complete a writing task to identify which of your procedures are successful and which should be replaced. Your writing journal is a good place to do this. If you regularly assess your process, you will develop procedures that help you become a more successful writer.

Figure 3
PROCESS LOG

Task _____

Date _____

To generate ideas, I did the following: _____
_____
_____

To produce a rough draft, I did the following: _____
_____
_____

To revise my draft, I did the following: _____
_____
_____
_____

To edit my draft, I did the following: _____
_____
_____
_____

These procedures worked well for me: _____
_____
_____

These procedures did not work well for me: _____
_____
_____

The next time I write, I will try these procedures: _____
_____
_____
_____

Using Reader Response Questionnaires

To help them decide what and how to revise, writers often ask reliable readers to respond to their drafts (see page 73). If you want to consider the opinions of readers when you make revision decisions, you can ask people to complete a questionnaire like the one in Figure 4. To make reader response as valuable as possible, remember the following points:

1. Be sure that the people who read your work are aware of the qualities of effective writing.

2. Be sure that the people who read your work are comfortable giving constructive criticism; do not ask someone to read your work who is reluctant to tell you when something is wrong.

3. Give your readers legible drafts.

4. If you have specific concerns about your draft, mention them to your readers and ask them to speak to those points.

5. Weigh out your readers' responses carefully—do not assume your

readers are always correct. If you are in doubt about the value of a response, ask your instructor or a writing center tutor.

6. Talk to your readers and ask them why they responded as they did.

7. Photocopy your draft so it can be read by more than one reader. Look for agreement in the readers' responses.

Figure 4
READER RESPONSE QUESTIONNAIRE

1. Can you easily tell what the thesis is? If so, what is that thesis?

_____

_____

2. Are you interested in reading about this thesis? Why or why not?

_____

_____

3. What do you like best about this essay?

_____

_____

4. Do any points go unproven or unsupported? If so, which ones?

_____

_____

5. Is there anything you do not understand? If so, what?

_____

_____

6. Is there anything so obvious it does not need to be stated? If so, what?

_____

_____

7. Does any detail stray from the thesis? If so, what?

_____

_____

8. Does the introduction engage your interest? Why or why not?

_____

_____

9. Is the conclusion satisfying? Why or why not?

_____

_____

10. Do you have any advice for the writer that was not covered by the previous questions?

_____

_____

Coping with Essay Examinations

Essay examinations are an important part of college life. The tips in this section may help you improve your performance on these tests. Of course, there is no substitute for thorough studying, so the tips only work if you are prepared. If you think you need to sharpen your study skills, visit your campus study skills center.

UNDERSTAND THE VALUE OF ANXIETY

Anxiety can keep you alert and focused so you perform well. Thus, if you are nervous before and during an exam, you should not be concerned. However, while a degree of anxiety will help you, too much can make you panicky and hurt your performance. To keep your anxiety at the appropriate level, use the test-taking strategies in this appendix.

HAVE A TEST-TAKING PLAN

A plan helps you keep your anxiety in check because it tells you what you will do first, second, third, and so forth. When you know how you will proceed, you minimize the anxiety and fear associated with the unknown. If you need a plan, try this:

1. Read through the entire test to get a sense of what is expected of you.

2. Decide how you will budget your time. If you have one hour to answer four questions, plan to spend fifteen minutes on each question. However, if some questions are worth more points than others, spend the most time on the questions worth the most points.

3. Plan your first answer with a scratch outline. Make a quick list of the points you will cover, and number them in the order you will write them up.

4. Write your first answer, using your scratch outline. Do not plan to revise; you may not have time.

5. Outline and write your next answer, and proceed in this manner until you have completed the test.

6. If you have time after answering all the questions, go back and revise as necessary.

ORGANIZE SIMPLY

Time is not on your side, so forget introductions and conclusions. Open with a sentence that reflects the question (your thesis) and then go on to make your points. For example, if the question is "Explain manifest destiny," begin this way: "Manifest destiny is. . . ."

ANSWER THE QUESTIONS YOU ARE SURE OF FIRST

While you are answering the questions you know, a portion of your brain will turn to the ones you are less certain of, and the answers you need may occur to you.

THINK POSITIVELY

Studies show that all things being equal, positive thinkers outperform negative thinkers.

PICTURE YOURSELF TAKING THE TEST

If you become overly anxious about tests, repeatedly picture yourself in the classroom, receiving the exam sheet, reading it over, writing scratch outlines, answering questions successfully, and feeling confident.

AVOID PADDING YOUR ANSWERS

Your instructor will recognize padding, that is, adding unrelated information because you do not know the correct answer. A busy instructor is likely to grow annoyed by padding, and you do not want to annoy the person giving you a grade.

IF YOU DO NOT KNOW THE ANSWER, GUESS

If you are lucky, you may get some points. Guessing is not the same as padding, however. Keep your answer, whether or not it is a guess, to the point.

IF YOU RUN OUT OF TIME, MAKE A LIST
OF THE POINTS YOU WOULD HAVE INCLUDED
IN YOUR ANSWER

Most instructors will give at least partial credit if you demonstrate your knowledge.

WEAR A WATCH

You need to keep track of the time so you know how long to spend on each answer.

IF YOU DO NOT UNDERSTAND A QUESTION,
ASK YOUR INSTRUCTOR FOR CLARIFICATION

You may not get help, but then again you may.

Index

Index